THE FUTURE
OF BUSINESS
REGULATION

THE FUTURE OF BUSINESS REGULATION

Private Action and

Public Demand

Murray L. Weidenbaum

A Division of American Management Associations

Library of Congress Cataloging in Publication Data

Weidenbaum, Murray L
  The future of business regulation.

  Includes index.
  1. Industry and state--United States. 2. Industry
--Social aspects--United States. I. Title.
HD3616.U46W453   338.973   79-4389
ISBN 0-8144-5521-2

First Printing

Preface

THE motivation for this book is the strong belief that the prospects for the American economy depend not so much on educating future generations of economists as on communicating to the current generation of citizens a better understanding of the full effects of citizens' actions on the private enterprise system. As is shown in detail, so many good intentions on the part of well-meaning citizens are frequently but unexpectedly translated into regulations that have extremely negative impacts on the basic functioning of the private enterprise system—to the detriment of the public.

The book lays out an ambitious agenda of voluntary steps by business, government, and private interest groups, all of which are designed to increase the ability of the business system to meet the needs of the public that business serves. But it will take a different climate of public opinion to convince each of those groups that those voluntary but difficult actions must be undertaken. Hopefully, the materials developed here will be used by a wide variety of communicators to achieve that shift in public opinion.

The most necessary improvement in public policy in this period of rising government involvement in the private sector can be summed up in an admonition to government decision makers: "Physician, heal thyself." Unlike a private business faced with unwilling customers that finds its sales plummeting, modern government does not seem to have the capacity to change its ways in response to citizen desires. The armies of bureaucrats employed by governments surely have the incentive to maintain the status quo and to forestall any attempts at reform. And legislatures, judging by their performance, are more responsive to the concentrated pressures of the specific groups that benefit from government programs than to the more generalized concern of the average citizen who bears the burden of big government.

Big government truly needs to administer to itself a carefully prescribed dose of self-restraint. Otherwise, aroused citizens will force on it a crash starvation diet which it would surely deserve.

The preparation of this book was supported by the Center for the Study of American Business at Washington University. The author is indebted to Ronald Penoyer for much helpful research and editorial assistance. Rachel Knipp carefully typed the drafts and final version of the manuscript. Lee Benham, Kenneth Chilton, Kenneth Shepsle, and Barry Weingast provided many useful comments and suggestions. The views expressed are, of course, entirely those of the author.

Murray L. Weidenbaum

Contents

1

The Problem of Government Encroachment on U.S. Business

The United States has discovered a new disease called "regulation." It is as prevalent as athlete's foot in a locker room.
Helen Hackman, M.D.
Director, Arlington County
Department of Human Resources

The morning alarm rings. John and Mary start another day in what will turn out to be a highly regulated existence.

The alarm clock that awakens them is run by electricity provided by a utility regulated by the Federal Energy Regulatory Commission and by state utility agencies. John then goes to the bathroom, where he uses a mouthwash and other products made by companies regulated by the Food and Drug Administration (FDA). He only mildly loses his temper trying to open a bottle of aspirin, which has the child-proof cap required by the Consumer Product Safety Commission (CPSC). In the kitchen Mary reaches for a box of cereal containing food processed by a firm subject to the regulations of the United States Department of Agriculture (USDA) and required to label its product under regulations of the Federal Trade Commission (FTC). John, who is under doctor's orders to limit his calorie intake, uses an artificial sweetener in his coffee. Since the banning of cyclamates by the FDA, he has switched to saccharin, but he is worried because that too is on the FDA's proposed ban list. All that is doing his ulcer no good.

As John and Mary are pulling their car out of the garage, the seat belt buzzer is sounding (courtesy of the National Highway Traffic Safety Administration). The car they are driving to work has cost them more than they would like to have paid because it contains a catalytic converter and other expensive devices stipulated by the Environmental Protection Agency (EPA). The car can use only unleaded gasoline (another government requirement). They drive at speeds regulated by state and municipal ordinances and subject to the federally mandated 55 miles an hour speed limit.

Mary enters the business office where she works, which is located in a building whose construction was repeatedly delayed before it met the Environmental Protection Agency's regulations and state and local building codes. She was hired after a suit was filed by the Equal Employment Opportunity Commission (EEOC), which had accused the firm of discrimination against women. During the course of the day, Mary provides information about the financial activities of her company to an investigator from the Securities and Exchange Commission (SEC), and she also fills out a variety of statistical forms for the Bureau of Census. In the personnel office she finds that she has lost her retirement benefits; the small company in which she is employed recently terminated its pension plan because of the onerous requirements imposed by the Internal Revenue Service and the Department of Labor under the Employee Retirement Income Security Act (ERISA).

John goes to the factory where he works under conditions negotiated by his union (chosen, after a prolonged strike, in an election supervised by the National Labor Relations

Board, or NLRB). The equipment he currently uses in his job is more cumbersome than it used to be, but it was selected in order to meet the requirements of the Occupational Safety and Health Administration (OSHA)—a government agency which could be returning any day for another surprise inspection. He works on materials shipped to his firm by companies under authority granted by government—the Interstate Commerce Commission (ICC, for rail and truck), the Civil Aeronautics Board (CAB, for air), and the Federal Maritime Commission (for sea).

During their lunch hour, John and Mary negotiate for a mortgage on the house they are buying with financing from a savings and loan association (regulated by the Federal Home Loan Bank Board), with a guarantee (subject to numerous, detailed regulations) by the Federal Housing Administration of the Department of Housing and Urban Development. If they had the time, they would also have liked to visit their commercial bank (regulated by the Federal Reserve System) to obtain a loan for the furniture they will need. But the paperwork requirements—involving truth in lending, equal credit opportunity, and several related credit rulings of the government—will force them to come back the next day.

At home in the evening, John, Mary, and their children watch commercial television, the programming and advertising of which are regulated by the Federal Communications Commission (FCC). Simultaneously, John is cleaning his shotgun (regulated by the Alcohol, Tobacco, and Firearms Bureau of the Treasury Department) and Mary is lighting up a cigarette, whose package label is mandated by the Surgeon General in the Department of Health, Education, and Welfare.

Watching, they are barely aware that they, in turn, are being watched over almost continuously by an imposing number and variety of regulatory agencies.

That scenario may be hypothetical, but each of the incidents in it occurs regularly in the lives of typical American citizens in the course of earning a livelihood in the business world and spending the earnings on the products that businesses make. The encroachment of government power in the private sector in recent years has been massive. Moreover, it has been, in the main, self-defeating. Despite the noble intentions, government intervention on an increasing scale has interfered with and inhibited the ability of the typical business enterprise to meet the needs of the consumer. Furthermore, the intervention has occurred in ways which have tended to minimize, rather than maximize, the achievement of the basic social objectives which have been the motivating force for the expansion of government involvement in private decision making.

The point that will be developed in this book involves far more than merely identifying the waste and inefficiency that often occur in the process of government regulation. If it were merely a matter of cost, the problem would be quite manageable. Rather, the fundamental concern is that the rapid and pervasive growth of government rules, regulations, prohibitions, and requirements is increasingly preventing the private enterprise system from delivering the rising standard of living and level of employment which the public has come to expect and which provides the basic political support for the future of the business system.

It has become fashionable in business circles to bemoan the coming decline of capitalism. Some outstanding conservative scholars have been writing about what they see as the impending disappearance of the corporate form of organization. That pessimistic outcome is not in keeping with the spirit of this book. This is not a plea for business executives to rend their garments, don sackcloth and ashes, and recite from Lamentations. On the other hand, a rosy forecast of an economic Valhalla in our time surely is not appropriate either.

Nor is this book going to take the often popular course of urging business firms to act "socially responsible" and adjust to the inevitable expansion of government intervention in the economy. It is not a matter of choosing the general welfare over the needs of the individual business firm. In practice, the two are so interdependent that to do harm to the typical business firm often detracts from the general welfare. Thus the plea of this book to reverse the current trend of ever-increasing government intervention in business decision making is made with an intent to enhance the general welfare.

The purpose here is to detail the nature of the fundamental problems that have arisen from proliferated government activity and then show both the desirability and the possibility of turning the tide. Surely, at least in the short run, the future is going to see more rather than less government regulation of business. But the course will be uneven, with a few dips and curves along the way. It would not be surprising if, a decade from now, the prospects for the private enterprise system in the United States were more favorable than they are today. That pleasant state of affairs, however, will not come about effortlessly. The first step is to understand the long-term effects of the continuation of recent trends and communicate that improved understanding to a wide audience of citizens, voters, taxpayers, and public and private decision makers.

It is important to appreciate the direct connection between extensive regulation by government in the first instance and the pleas for more detailed government intervention in business that follow. When government policies increase the cost of private production, they can create pressure for even greater government involvement in wage and price decisions. When excessive government regulation of business reduces the ability of and incentive for business to engage in technological innovation, the economy suffers a further reduction in its capability to achieve such important national objectives as greater job opportunities, rising standards of living, and an improved quality of life.

And when government policies sharply curtail the ability of the private sector to generate adequate savings to finance economic growth, not only is the government looked upon as the banker of last resort but the basic vitality of the business system is called into question. Public dissatisfaction with business performance is increased in the process. In turn, that sets the scene for another round of government involvement ranging from proposals to nationalize specific industries to subsidizing others (always, of course, with still more restrictions and federal regulations). Energy is a clear example of the phenomenon, and the pharmaceutical and health care industries may be on the verge of becoming another. It is a truly vicious cycle. The expansion of government involvement is self-reinforcing. The result can often be a downward spiral in the progress of the overall economy.

To be sure, not all government regulation is undesirable, nor can all of the shortcomings of the American business system be attributed to government interference. It must be recognized that impetus for the expanded government actions is being provided by a variety of citizen groups truly concerned with various shortcomings in our national life. In many cases the increasing regulation reflects public and congressional knowledge that traditional federal and state-local programs have not been effective. The new wave of regulation is also reinforced by the belief that the private sector itself is responsible for many of the problems facing society: pollution, discrimination in employment, unsafe products, unhealthy working environments, misleading financial reporting, and so forth. In that view, voluntary responses by business have not been and will not be entirely satisfactory.

Nevertheless, as will be shown in detail in the chapters that follow, the rising tide of regulation has become a major barrier to productive economic activity. The costs arising from government regulation are basic: (1) the cost to the taxpayer for supporting a galaxy of government regulators, (2) the cost to the consumer in the form of higher prices to cover the added expense of producing goods and services under government regulations, (3) the cost to the worker in the form of jobs eliminated by government regulation, (4) the cost to the economy resulting from the loss of smaller enterprises which cannot afford to meet the onerous burdens of government regulations, and (5) the cost to society as a whole as a result of a reduced flow of new and better products and a less rapid rise in the standard of living. In a fundamental way, albeit unintentionally, the increasing power assumed by government over business often results in a diminution of business performance. It is not mere coincidence; in good measure, it is cause and effect.

The final sections of this book advocate a sensible balance in government action based on the obvious and necessary assumption that we are not a nation of anarchists. Business management, employees, and consumers share a common set of values and such long-term interests as a rising living standard, higher employment, less inflation, and a cleaner and healthier environment, although they may differ on the means of achieving those goals. All those groups in general believe that government should set rules for society. Surely, there *are* very important functions for government to perform. It is the responsibility of government to provide for the national defense as well as for internal law enforcement. It is the function of the government to provide the common systems—airports, seaports, and highways, to cite a few obvious examples—which are necessary for private individuals and private enterprise to function. But that position does not justify government closely intervening in *every* aspect of society. Moreover, when government actions become so detailed and poorly designed that they interfere with the basic functioning of society, it is indeed high time to set about the essential task of reform.

There is a need to develop some principles of business-government relations. As an initial attempt, here is a simple set of goals which need to be developed more fully: (1) to support government activities that, on balance, benefit society and then improve government's ability to carry them out and (2) to identify government activities that on balance harm society and then reform or eliminate them. That approach is not a knee-jerk defense of the status quo. Neither is it an automatic prescription for smaller government—or for the reverse. Rather, it is an approach which avoids taking doctrinaire positions by looking at the specific effects that flow from individual government actions. In some cases, following the twin set of goals may result in expanding certain government activities and restraining others.

In any event, it would be futile to advocate a return to the status quo ante. Public concern with environmental, safety, equity, and similar matters remains strong. It is not the ends but the means used which in practice may be changed substantially. One of the necessary tasks is to encourage the so-called and self-appointed public interest groups to undergo a fundamental metamorphosis. The public, the media, and government decision makers need to realize that those groups are prevented by their *limited* viewpoints from effectively representing the *totality* of the public interest. The problem is not venality, but the belief that they, and they alone, do represent the public interest.

In the public arena, those groups possess great power. Large segments of the media, as well as many legislators, defer to the representatives of the public interest groups because they automatically view the groups as the underdogs in disagreements with such other segments of society as business firms and government agencies. That simple-minded attitude also often results in the people who disagree with the public interest groups being portrayed in an unsympathetic light. Opposition to Ralph Nader on a specific issue should not inevitably be taken as provoked by some special interest opposed to the public welfare. It may just happen that, on occasion, Nader is wrong in interpreting the ultimate effect of a proposal on the consumer.

As, or if, those powerful interest groups acquire a greater economic understanding, the prospects for an enlightened public policy toward business should tend to improve substantially. And that desirable situation is likely to be hastened by our forcing them to maintain the same high standards of accuracy and fairness that they expect of others. In that regard, consider the following statement by two key officials of the National Council of Churches: "The movement for corporate responsibility . . . means that corporate decision makers should begin to consider the social implications of their decisions as carefully and with as much weight as they do the economic. It says that life and death are more important than profit and loss." [1] Personally, I can think of no instance in which a company deliberately chose "profit" over "life and death." Such triumphs of the heart over the mind must be labeled and treated as such—unhelpful contributions to serious discourse on important topics. Responsibility is a dual affair, and the attackers of the corporate system need to understand that if they wish to be taken seriously.

After all, it is intriguing that the so-called corporate activists seem to view the corporation as both venal and omnipotent. Many of the critics of the American business system gladly accept the accomplishments, the goods and services produced by the corporation, but they reject the values that have been followed in achieving those results. They ignore the role of material incentives in obtaining desired material benefits. They seem to act as though the corporation could continue to produce all of the material abundance at least as effectively as it now is doing while simultaneously turning its efforts to a host and variety of social and noneconomic concerns.

Much of the current discussion about the "legitimacy of the corporation" ignores the firm basis of that "legitimacy": the fact that the modern business is demonstrably the most effective vehicle for producing goods and services, creating jobs and incomes, and thus raising society's living standards. Certainly, the abuses which have been revealed need to be acknowledged and eliminated, but they should not obscure the basic accomplishments of the American corporation.

Finally, we must remind people of something so obvious that they often overlook it: when we examine the various nations of the world, it is apparent that those that provide their citizens with a greater degree of personal freedom are precisely those that have a large and strong private sector. The close correspondence between economic freedom and personal freedom is not accidental; the societies that have a large and independent business system have avoided the concentration of power that results in a totalitarian state. The data developed by Freedom House clearly illustrate this point. Each year that organization ranks the nations of the world according to the degree of political rights enjoyed by their citizens, from 1 (most free) to 7 (least free). In the case of Europe, for example, every capitalist nation is ranked in categories 1 or 2—most free. In striking contrast, each of the Communist nations is shown in categories 6 or 7—least free.[2]

Thus the concern with the future of our economic system may be seen as a reflection of a more basic desire to maintain and strengthen the free and voluntary society of which the economy is a vital but only a constituent part. Boiled down to its essence, economic freedom is inseparable from political freedom. We foster one as we pursue the other.

References

1. Frank White and Tim Smith, "Corporate Responsibility and the Church," in S. Prakash Sethi, ed., *The Unstable Ground: Corporate Social Policy in a Dynamic Society* (Los Angeles: Melville, 1974), p. 514. Frank White is director, Corporate Information Center, National Council of Churches, New York City, and Tim Smith is executive secretary, Interfaith Committee on Social Responsibility in Investments, National Council of Churches.
2. "The Comparative Survey of Freedom—VIII," *Freedom at Issue*, January–February 1978.

2

The Growing Array of Government Interventions

The might and power of the Federal Government have no equal. . . . Men of goodwill, not evil ones only, invent, under feelings of urgency, new and different procedures that have an awful effect on the citizen.
William O. Douglas
Hannah v. Larche (1960)

IN the area of government intervention, as in many others, business is the quintessential middleman. It is the consumer that bears the ultimate effects. The phenomenon is most clear and visible in the area of automobile regulation. The newly produced automobile in the United States carries a load of equipment which the federal government has mandated must be installed. Those gadgets, which have a variety of consumer acceptance levels, range from the catalytic converter designed to reduce air pollution (average cost of $119.20) to head restraints ($25.80) to a required windshield wiping system ($1.25). The various effects which those and other forms of regulation have on business and the economy fall into three broad categories: direct, indirect, and induced.

THE DIRECT, OR FIRST-ORDER, EFFECTS

All in all, there was approximately $666 in government-mandated safety and environment control equipment in the typical 1978 passenger automobile. For the 10 million cars sold that year, that amounted to $6.7 billion of higher auto prices paid by the American consumer. Table 1 shows how highly detailed federal intervention in the auto industry since 1968 has substantially raised the retail price of every automobile.

The $6.7 billion automobile price increase, although not to be dismissed lightly, is only one example of the pervasive impacts of regulatory activities on the day-to-day operations of business. Big Brother involves himself in even the most trivial decisions of a company. In-Line, Inc., a North Carolina construction firm, has reported the insistence of a federal safety inspector that it provide a portable toilet for its workers who were digging a tunnel under a highway. The company argued in vain with the Occupational Safety and Health Administration that the men never complained about using the toilet at a filling station 50 yards away. The story's point, of course, is simply this: The regulators (and the rules they were enforcing) were blind to, or at least unmindful of, the particular situation at hand; the requirement was arbitrarily imposed without regard to the desires or demands of individual people or individual businesses. In the process, time, effort, and money were expended unnecessarily in compliance.

Another example, but on a much larger scale, is that of the electric utilities, which were required, only a few years ago, by the environmental agencies to shift from coal to oil in their production of power in order to reduce pollution but were subsequently required by the energy agencies to shift back to the use of coal to reduce the importation of oil. Businesses therefore face an additional problem, since just as a company learns to adjust to one set of regulators and their regulations, a different set of regulators and regulations is imposed by Congress.

Time magazine may have overstated the case in its January 2, 1978 issue when it reported that "the growing number of federal rules and regulations . . . seem to float out from Washington as

Table 1. Increase in retail price of automobiles due to federal requirements.

Year of Regulation	Action	Estimated Current Cost
1968	Seat and shoulder belts; standards for exhaust emissions	$ 47.84
1968–1969	Windshield defrosting systems; door latches	14.53
1969	Head restraints and accessories	27.48
1970	Reflective devices and further emission standards	14.77
1968–1970	Ignition locking and buzzing systems	12.75
1971	Fuel evaporative systems	28.33
1972	Improved exhaust emissions and warranty changes; seat belt warning system	42.37
1972–1973	Exterior protection	95.29
1973	Reduced flammability materials	8.72
1969–1973	Improved side door strength	20.85
1974	Interlock system and improved exhaust emissions	133.50
1975	Additional safety features and catalytic converter	146.66
1976	Hydraulic brakes, improved bumpers, removal of interlock system	41.54
1977	Leak-resistant fuel system	21.25
1978	Redesign of emissions controls	9.99
	Total	$665.87

Source: Center for the Study of American Business

casually as children blow soap bubbles," yet the overstatement may not have been as great as it seems at first glance. In the five-year period 1974 to 1978, Congress enacted the following 25 wide-ranging additions to the arsenal of regulatory power over business:

The Toxic Substances Control Act

The Surface Mining Control and Reclamation Act

The Export Administration Act (imposing restrictions on complying with the Arab boycott of Israel)

The Business Payments Abroad Act (providing for up to $1 million in penalties for bribing foreign officials)

The Redlining Disclosure Act

The Magnuson-Moss Warranty Improvement Act

The Antitrust Amendments of 1976 (providing for class action suits by state attorneys general and requiring large companies to notify the Department of Justice of planned mergers and acquisitions)

The Hazardous Materials Transportation Act

The Commodity Futures Trading Commission Act

The Energy Policy and Conservation Act

The Community Reinvestment Act of 1977 (encouraging financial institutions to meet local credit needs)

The Resource Conservation and Recovery Act (licensing waste haulers and setting record-keeping requirements)

Securities and Exchange Amendments of 1975 (eliminating fixed commissions for stock brokers)

The Fair Marketing Practices Act (regulating dealings between oil companies and their dealers)

The United Nations Participation Act Amendment (giving the President authority to terminate imports of Rhodesian chrome)

The Saccharin Study and Labeling Act (requiring labeling of food products containing saccharin)

The Fair Labor Standards Amendments of 1977 (raising the minimum wage)

The 1978 Amendments to the Age Discrimination in Employment Act (raising the permissible mandatory retirement age from 65 to 70 for most employees)

The Fair Debt Collection Practices Act (the first nationwide control of debt collection agencies)

The Medical Device Amendments of 1976 (extending premarket controls over medical instruments)

The Employee Retirement Income Security Act

The Real Estate Settlement Procedures Act
Little Cigars Act
Egg Research and Consumer Information Act
Fishery Conservation and Management Act

When we try to add up the activities of the federal regulatory agencies (comprehensive data on the growing state and local regulators are not available), we find that the operating budgets are on a steep upward trajectory. The budgeted $4.8 billion to run the various federal regulatory bureaus in fiscal 1979 represents a 115 percent expansion from the $2.2 billion level of fiscal 1974. There are few parts of the private sector that have recorded such gains in the same five-year period. Government regulation of business literally has become a major growth area of the American economy.[1]

Government imposition of socially desirable requirements on business through the regulatory process may appear at first to be an inexpensive way to achieve national objectives. It would seem to represent no significant burden on the consumer. However, the public does not get a free or even a low-cost lunch when government imposes requirements on private industry. In large measure, the costs of government regulation show up in higher prices of the goods and services that consumers buy. Those higher prices represent the hidden tax imposed on the public by government regulation, and the imposition of the hidden tax offsets some of the formal tax cuts that Congress has passed in recent years. In effect, the real level of federal taxation—the government burden imposed on the public—is higher than is generally realized.

There have been several efforts to quantify the growing costs that result from the increasing array of regulation.[2] A study in Colorado found that changing regulatory requirements and practices had added $1,500 to $2,000 to the cost of the typical new house built between 1970 and 1975. The added cost reflected higher water and sewer tap fees, increased permit fees, greater school and park land dedication requirements, and new mandates for wider and thicker streets, fences, underground storm sewers, and environmental impact studies.

Two other investigations show very similar cost increases. A study covering 21 residential development projects in the New Jersey Coastal Zone estimated the direct regulatory expenses for a single-family house at $1,600 during the period 1972–1975. The costs covered some 38 separately required permits including preliminary plan, performance improvement bond, sewer plan, tree removal permit, final plans review, road drainage permit, and coastal area facilities permit.

A study in St. Louis County, Missouri, of the increase in lot development and homebuilding costs during 1970–1975 found that the expense of meeting new government requirements came to $1,600 to $2,500 for a typical 1,600-square-foot house on a 10,000-square-foot lot. The new governmentally imposed requirements included street lighting, greater collector street widths, higher permit and inspection fees, added features to electrical systems, and smoke detectors.

By using the midpoint of the range of cost estimates for housing regulation ($2,000) and applying it to the 2 million new homes being built a year, the added cost to the homebuyer amounts to $4 billion annually.

THE INDIRECT, OR SECOND-ORDER, EFFECTS

But examination of the visible cost to the taxpayer ($4.8 billion) or the direct cost to the motorist ($6.7 billion) or the direct cost to the homeowner ($4.0 billion) is merely the starting point; it reflects only the initial or first-order effects of government regulation. The indirect or second-order effects necessary to change a company's way of doing business in order to comply with federal government directives are truly huge.

One indirect cost of government regulation is the growing paperwork imposed on business firms: the expensive and time-consuming process of submitting reports, making applications, filling out questionnaires, replying to orders and directives, and preparing court appeals resulting from some of the regulatory hearings. There are over 4,400 different types of federally approved forms, in addition to tax and banking forms, and individuals and business firms spend over 143 million man-hours a year filling them out. The 71,500 man-years involved is the equivalent of a small army or the total employment of a company such as the General Dynamics Corporation.

One example of the paperwork burden is regulation Z of the Federal Reserve System, which was promulgated to carry out the Truth-in-Lending Act. That one regulation requires at least fourteen separate disclosures:

The date of the transaction
The annual percentage interest rate
The payment schedule
The amount or method of calculating any delinquency charge
A description of the security interest and collateral
The method of calculating the rebate on unearned interest in
    the event of prepayment
The cash price
The down payment
The unpaid balance of the cash price
Other charges, itemized
The unpaid balance and amount financed
The finance charge
The deferred payment price
Credit insurance authorization

The rising paperwork and ancillary requirements of government agencies inevitably produce a lengthening regulatory lag, a delay that often runs into years and is a costly drain on the time and budgets of private managers as well as public officials. Ten years ago, the director of planning of the Irvine Company, a West Coast land developer, obtained in 90 days what was then called zoning for a typical residential development. A decade later, the company received what is now called an entitlement to build for one of its developments, but only following two years of intensive work by a specialized group within the company's planning department aided by the public affairs staff. That may not be too surprising, in view of remarks made by the Undersecretary of the Department of Housing and Urban Development. The federal official recalled a conversation that he had with a

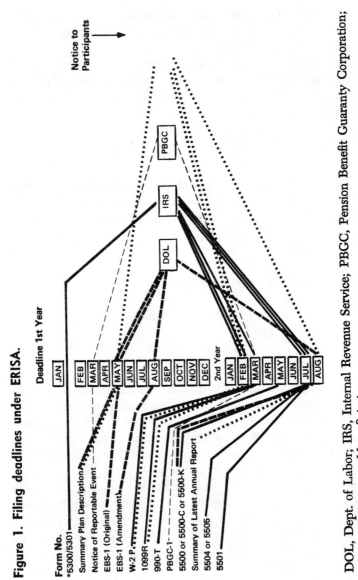

Figure 1. Filing deadlines under ERISA.

DOL, Dept. of Labor; IRS, Internal Revenue Service; PBGC, Pension Benefit Guaranty Corporation; P&B, participants and beneficiaries.
Source: Commission on Federal Paperwork.

county commissioner when he was a builder in Florida. The commissioner was explaining his "pinball technique" for protecting the environment: "When a builder comes in with a certain project, I just bounce him around from one department to another." [3]

Some of the government's paperwork requirements conjure up visions of Rube Goldberg machines. For an example see Figure 1, which shows the multiple filing deadlines for the various reporting forms generated pursuant to the Employee Retirement Income Security Act (ERISA, the pension regulations authorized by the Congress in 1974). The pension reform paperwork burden is neither an exception nor the final word in terms of federal impositions on the time and resources of the private sector. For example, the information now being required under the Toxic Substances Control Act is proliferating rapidly and the Hazardous Materials Transportation Act is spawning another generation of paperwork.

In 1976, the Dow Chemical Company attempted to estimate the total costs it incurred in complying with federal government regulations. The measurable expenses came to $186 million, a 27 percent increase from the 1975 total. To be fair, the company stated that many of the costs, $103 million (or 55 percent), were necessary for the safety and protection of workers, customers, and the public at large. The remainder were defined as expenditures which were beyond good scientific manufacturing, business, or personnel practices or those in which the regulations duplicate the efforts of other agencies.[4]

One of the hidden aspects of regulation is an adverse effect on the company's ability to increase production and employment. Dow maintains that regulatory roadblocks and delay eventually led to its decision, in January 1977, to cancel plans for building a $300 million petrochemical complex in California to meet growing West Coast demand for the company's products and services. According to Paul Oreffice, president of Dow Chemical Company, "After more than two years and costs exceeding $4 million for an environmentally sound project, we hadn't even reached first base in the regulatory red tape maze."

When the project was canceled, Dow had obtained only 4 of

the 65 permits it needed from various federal, state, local, and regional regulatory agencies involved in review of the proposed project. Economists Eugene Bardach and Lucian Pugliaresi have vividly described the problems of the federally required environmental impact statements (EIS): "The EIS process . . . continues to be used as an instrument of legal and political warfare. . . . Environmentalist critics thus exploit the opportunities for harassment and legal delay." At times, moreover, the delay in the EIS process may be compounded by sheer bureaucratic inefficiency. In the case of the proposed nuclear power plant at Seabrook, New Hampshire, a federal appeals court ruled in February 1978 that the EPA had failed to follow its own administrative procedures in assessing the project's environmental impact. The court ordered a delay in construction in order to permit EPA to repeat the review process.[5]

The most serious second-order effects of government regulation are losses of productivity. In some cases they are dramatic. In 1976, coal production averaged 13.6 tons per man per day, a 32 percent decline from the 1969 figure of 19.9 and a sharp reversal from the growth in labor productivity during the preceding seven years. There is widespread agreement that the basic causes were the changes in mining procedures made by the coal companies to comply with the Coal Mine Health and Safety Act of 1969.[6]

In a pioneering study, Edward F. Denison of the Brookings Institution estimated that business productivity in 1975 was 1.4 percent lower than it otherwise would have been owing to the total costs of meeting governmental pollution and job safety requirements.[7] One percent may not seem like much, until we realize that the total annual gain in productivity experienced by the American economy may only be 2 to 3 percent. That productivity loss amounts to a reduction of about $20 billion in the annual level of the gross national product.

Moreover, we cannot always assume that the loss of private productivity is offset by an improvement in some area of social concern. For example, Armco Steel Corporation was required to install special scrubbing equipment at one of its plants to reduce the emission of visible iron oxide dust. The scrubber does succeed in capturing 21.2 pounds per hour of the pollutant. However, it is run by a 1,020-horsepower electric motor. In producing the power for that motor, the electric utility's plant spews out 23.0 pounds per hour of sulfur and nitrogen oxides and other gaseous pollutants. Thus, even though Armco is meeting government regulations on visible emissions, the air is actually 1.8 pounds per hour dirtier because of the government's regulatory requirement.[8]

The Armco case is no isolated example. Scrubbers are increasingly becoming required equipment of electric utilities that are attempting to comply with EPA regulations. The federal agencies, by being unable or unwilling to consider the adverse but *indirect* effects of their actions, are likely to produce more instances in which unintended but undesirable side effects swamp the benefits. Consider the sad story of the Pennsylvania Power Company. That utility has a new 825-megawatt complex that utilizes scrubbers. In extracting the pollutants from coal, it produces 18,000 tons of sludge a day. To dispose of the sludge, the company has been forced to build a 350-foot-high dam, the largest earth and rock embankment east of the Mississippi River. Behind the dam, there is now a lake of sludge, which already covers 900 acres in a picturesque valley of Western Pennsylvania!

Government regulation can also have strongly adverse effects on employment, except, that is, for the expansion in corporate legal and reporting staffs. That has been demonstrated by the minimum wage law: teenagers have increasingly been priced out of the labor market. One recent study has shown that the 1966 increase in the statutory minimum wage resulted in teenage employment in the United States being 225,000 lower in 1972 than it would otherwise have been.[9]

It is difficult, of course, to obtain an aggregate measure of the total cost involved in complying with governmental regulations. A pioneering effort was made at the Center for the Study of American Business at Washington University in St. Louis. Robert DeFina culled from the available literature the more reliable estimates of the costs of specific regulatory programs. By using a conservative estimating procedure, he put the various dollar figures on a consistent basis and aggregated the results for 1976 (see Table 2). He found the total annual cost of federal regulation to be approximately $66 billion, consisting of $3 billion of taxpayer costs to operate the regulatory agencies and $63 billion (or 20 times as much) for business to comply with the regulations.[10] Thus, on the average, each dollar that Congress appropri-

Table 2. Annual cost of federal regulation, by area, 1976 (millions of dollars).

Area	Administrative Cost	Compliance Cost	Total
Consumer safety and health	$1,516	$ 5,094	$ 6,610
Job safety and working conditions	483	4,015	4,498
Energy and the environment	612	7,760	8,372
Financial regulation	104	1,118	1,222
Industry specific	484	19,919	20,403
Paperwork	*	25,000	25,000
Total	$3,199	$62,906	$66,105

* Included in other categories
Source: Center for the Study of American Business

ates for regulation imposes an additional $20 of costs on the private sector of the economy. The $66 billion cost of regulation is equivalent to 3.6 percent of the Gross National Product, or $307 for every man, woman, and child living in the United States in 1976.

If we apply the same multiplier of 20 (between the amounts budgeted for regulatory activities and the private cost of compliance) to the budget figures which are available for more recent years, we can come up with more current approximations of the private sector's cost of compliance. Table 3 shows the costs arising from federal regulation of business (both the expenses of the regulatory agencies themselves and the costs they induce in the private sector) rising to a total of $102.7 billion in 1979, or almost $500 per capita.

Table 3. Estimated cost of federal regulation of business (Fiscal years, in billions of dollars).

	1977	1978	1979
Administrative costs	$ 3.7	$ 4.5	$ 4.8
Compliance costs	75.4	92.2	97.9
Total	$79.1	$96.7	$102.7

Source: Center for the Study of American Business

INDUCED, OR THIRD-ORDER, EFFECTS

The most fundamental impacts of government intervention on the corporation are what we can call the third-order effects. They are the actions that the firm takes to respond to the direct and indirect effects of regulation. The responses often include such negative effects as cutting back on new capital formation because of the diversion of funds to meet government-mandated social requirements. The basic functioning of the business system is adversely affected by the cumulative impacts of government actions, notably in the pace of innovation, the ability to finance growth, and ultimately the firm's capability to perform its central role of producing goods and services for the consumer. Those difficult-to-measure impacts may, in the long run, far outweigh the more measurable costs resulting from the imposition of government influence on private sector decision making.

Government regulation affects the prospects for economic growth and productivity by levying a claim for a rising share of new investments in an industry (technically, capital formation). That is most evident in the environmental and safety areas, in which government-mandated outlays account for almost one-tenth of new capital formation. Moreover, available evidence indicates that the percentage may be growing. With reference to the Labor Department's proposed noise standards, the troubled steel industry estimates that conversion to the engineering controls desired by OSHA would cost approximately $1.2 million for each affected steelworker. The industry claims that it can provide better protection for only $42 per employee. That would include $10 for ear protectors, $12 for noise monitoring, and $20 for audiometric testing.[11]

The capital formation situation is worsened by the accelerated rate at which existing manufacturing facilities are being closed down because the rapidly rising costs of meeting government regulations make them no longer economically viable. Several hundred foundries in the United States were closed down during 1968–1975 in part because they could not meet requirements such as those imposed by the Environmental Protection Agency and the Occupational Safety and Health Administration.

The government decision-making process can have other adverse effects on capital formation by introducing uncertainty about the future of regulations governing the introduction of new processes and products. An example is furnished in a November 1975 report by a task force of the President's Energy Resources Council dealing with the possibility of developing a new synthetic fuel industry. With reference to the National Environmental Policy Act of 1969, the task force stated that the major uncertainty was the length of time that a project would be delayed pending the issuance of an environmental impact statement that would stand up in court. The task force pointed out, "The cost of such delays (construction financing and inflated raw materials and labor costs) is an obvious potential hazard to any synfuels project." In evaluating the overall impact of government regulatory activity, the task force concluded, "In summary, some of these requirements could easily hold up or permanently postpone any attempt to build and operate a synthetic fuels plant." [12]

Meanwhile, it is becoming increasingly difficult for U.S. companies to move ahead with building conventional energy facilities. It took the Standard Oil Company of Ohio (Sohio) more than four years to obtain the 703 permits required to construct a terminal and a pipeline from Long Beach, California, to Midland, Texas. Many of the regulatory obstacles were environmentally related; they varied from air quality approval to California Coastal Zone permits. Whenever changes in the project were made to meet one agency's regulatory requirements, the company was required to resubmit applications to agencies that already had approved their aspects of the project. Sohio discovered that each of three different agencies had required that all other permits be granted before it could consider the company's application. Obviously, it was impossible for each of the three to be the last to grant a permit. Fortunately, Sohio was able to negotiate a compromise.[13]

At the present time, there is great concern among business planners that the regulations issued by the EPA under the 1977 Amendments to the Clean Air Act will slow, if not halt, industrial expansion in many parts of the United States. Under those regulations, each state must submit detailed plans which provide for stringent regulation of any major buildings that "emit or may emit any air pollutants." Failure to win EPA approval will result in an absolute prohibition of any new industrial construction in that state.[14]

The rapid expansion of government regulation of business is also slowing down the rate of innovation and scientific progress in the United States. The effect on research and development can be measured in many ways. In real terms (constant 1972 dollars), private sector R&D in the United States, which rose at an annual rate of over 7 percent in the period 1953–1967, has been increasing at a more modest 2 percent a year since that time. The employment of scientists and engineers in industry in 1975 was lower than in 1968 by 1,031,000 versus 1,046,000. That compares with a 19 percent increase in the 1960–1965 period. In 1973, the Patent Office issued fewer patents to U.S. nationals than in 1963, but patents issued to foreign nationals more than doubled during the same decade. All those are measures of stagnation or worse in our commitment of resources to technological innovation at a time when expenditures in most other sectors of the economy are growing.

One harmful but overlooked effect of government regulation is a reduced rate of introduction of new products and improved production processes. The longer it takes for an innovation to be approved by a government agency—or the more costly the approval procedures—the less likely it is that the new product or process will be introduced. In any event, innovation will be delayed. As William Carey of the American Association for the Advancement of Science has stated, "Government may imagine that it is neutral toward the rate and quality of technological risk-taking, but it is not. . . . Regulatory policies aimed at the public interest rarely consider impacts on innovation." [15]

As a result in large part of the stringent drug approval regulations, the United States is no longer the leader in introducing new medicines. We were the thirtieth country to approve the antiasthma drug metaproterenol, the thirty-second to approve the antituberculosis drug rifampin, the sixty-fourth to approve the antiallergenic drug cromolyn, and the one hundred sixth to approve the antibacterial drug co-trimaxazole. Professor William Wardell of the University of Rochester School of Medicine has shown that the slowdown has not provided compensating advantages to Americans by keeping out unsafe drugs. He made a detailed comparison between the United States and Great Britain in recent years. Dr. Wardell did point out that British patients suffered "more toxicity" due to new drugs than did patients in this country, as could have been anticipated from the fact that more new drugs were introduced in England. However, he found that the total burden of drug toxicity was "extremely small" and far smaller than the "clearly discernible" benefits from introducing useful new drugs sooner than in the United States. [16]

On occasion the regulators seem to have the private sector scared. In August 1975 the National Cancer Institute reported that the solvent trichlorethylene, known as TCE, might be a possible cause of cancer. TCE at the time was used in decaffeinated coffee. It seems that the government used a generous dose of the chemical on the test animals—the equivalent of a person's drinking 50 million cups of decaffeinated coffee every day for an entire lifetime. But did the industry laugh at that example of governmental nonsense? Hardly. With the cyclamate episode still firmly in mind and a saccharin ban being seriously considered, one major producer quickly changed to another chemical.[17]

In addition to the foolishness and uneconomical effects that can flow from government regulation, consideration must be given to the arbitrary power exercised by the personnel of regulatory agencies. For example, many people are outraged by the arbitrary no-knock powers of federal investigative agencies, yet they ignore the no-knock power used by federal agencies in their regulation of private business. The limitations (use of search warrants) imposed by the Supreme Court on OSHA's activities in industry in May 1978, however, can be seen as a favorable trend in the limitation of regulatory powers. Nonetheless, the awesome power exercised by government regulators often goes unappreciated by the public as well as by the regulators themselves. The case of the ban on spray adhesives (a type of art supply) is worthy of some attention.

On the surface, the ban appears to have been at most only a matter of excessive caution on the part of the Consumer Product Safety Commission. On August 20, 1973, the commission banned, as an imminent hazard, certain brands of aerosol spray adhesives commonly used to attach multicolored foil paper to posters. Its decision was based primarily on the preliminary findings of one academic researcher that the sprays could cause birth defects if used by pregnant women. After more careful research failed to corroborate the initial report, the commission lifted the ban on March 1, 1974. Why mention this case? Depriving artists of spray adhesives for less than seven months does not seem to be too harsh in view of the desire to avoid serious threats to human health. In fact, the admission of error on the part of the commission is commendable. Prompt rescission of the initial action would seem to be unprecedented.

But there is more to the story. According to a survey by researchers at the New York State Department of Health and the Albany Medical College, at least nine pregnant women who had used the spray adhesives reacted to the news of the commission's initial decision by undergoing abortions for fear of producing babies with birth defects. Unlike the regulatory commission, those women could not reverse their decisions.[18]

To the extent that management attention is diverted from product development, production, and marketing concerns to meeting governmentally imposed social requirements, a significant but subtle bureaucratization of corporate activity will result. In the employee pension area, for example, the federal government enacted the Employee Retirement Income Security Act of 1974 (ERISA). The intervention shifted much of the concern of the management of pension funds from maximizing the return on the contributions to following a more cautious approach of minimizing the likelihood that the fund managers will be criticized or even sued for their investment decisions. It thus becomes safer—although not necessarily more desirable to the employees covered—for the pension managers to keep more detailed records of their deliberations, to hire more outside experts (so that the responsibility can be diluted), and to avoid innovative investments. The federal rules also tend to make the pension fund manager unwilling to invest in other than blue-chip stocks, and they thereby deprive smaller, newer, and riskier enterprises of an important source of venture capital.

From the experience with pension fund regulation, we can see that the nation is paying yet another price for the expansion of government power: the attenuation of the risk-bearing and entrepreneurial characteristics of the private enterprise system which have contributed so effectively to rapid rates of innovation, productivity, growth, and progress. The ultimate negative impact on the business system that results from government intervention is the abandonment of specific activities and entire enterprises. Although that surely was not the intention, the advent of ERISA has led to the termination of numerous pension plans, especially in the case of smaller companies.

"There's no question that the new pension law has resulted in pension plan termination, sometimes three or four times the normal rate," states Warren Winer, director of retirement plans administration at General American Life Insurance Co. Mr. Winer reported that 10 percent of the more than 2,000 small-business plans that had been covered by his company were abandoned in 1975. The trend has continued on a national scale. The Pension Benefit Guaranty Corporation, the federal agency created by ERISA, reported that 7,300 pension plans were terminated in 1976, an 84 percent increase over 1975.[19]

The ERISA situation also illustrates the cycle of government intervention. To the extent that federal regulation reduces the coverage of private pension plans, we can expect increased pressures for greater benefits under the government's social insurance and welfare programs. It is ironic to note that the Social Security program would not come close to meeting the requirements imposed on private pension plans by ERISA.

SUMMARY

When the three categories of regulatory effects set forth here are viewed together, it is difficult to dispute Justice Douglas's remark, quoted at the beginning of this chapter, that "the might and power of the Federal Government have no equal." Further, the consequences of that power must be given new and discerning attention—not only by government itself and its regulators and by American businesses but also by the American public in general.

The first-order effects of regulation—the direct costs incurred by American business firms in complying with the directives of regulatory agencies at all levels of government—are becoming larger and more acute. As shown, those costs amount to billions of dollars annually, and they seem bound to increase. The second-order effects—indirect costs incurred by private companies as the companies change their basic ways of doing business to survive in the expanding labyrinth of government regulations—are even more burdensome. The vast amount of time and energy poured into paperwork and the subsequent slowdown of productive effort are so pervasive that they are difficult for the average citizen to comprehend. And on top of all that, there are third-order effects: the cumulative adverse results of regulation on industry's pace of innovation and development, ability to finance growth, and capability to perform the *basic* function of producing goods and services. Thus the ultimate costs of excessive government involvement in the economy can be seen in the factories that do not get built, the jobs that do not get created, the goods and services that do not get produced, and the incomes that are not generated.

The point that must be emphasized, therefore, is not that the plight of American business is severe, but rather that it is the American citizen—every one of us—who ultimately pays the heavy costs of government intervention.

References

1. See Murray L. Weidenbaum, *The Impacts of Government Regulation,* Working Paper No. 32 (St. Louis: Washington University Center for the Study of American Business, 1978).
2. Bickert, Browne, Coddington, and Associates, *An Analysis of the Impact of State and Local Government Intervention on the Home Building Process in Colorado, 1970–1975* (Denver: Colorado Association for Housing and Building, 1976); Dan K. Richardson, *The Cost of Environmental Protection: Regulating Housing Development in the Coastal Zone* (New Brunswick, N.J.: Center for Urban Policy Research, 1976); Real Estate Research Corporation, *New Home Construction Cost Increase, St. Louis County, Missouri* (St. Louis: Home Builders Association of Greater St. Louis, 1975).
3. Cited in "National Builders' Conference Debates Reasons for Sharp Increases in Housing Costs," *St. Louis Post-Dispatch,* September 11, 1977.
4. "Dow Reports Excessive Regulatory Costs," *News Release* (Midland, Mich.: Dow Chemical Co., March 5, 1977); *The Impact of Government Regulation on the Dow Chemical Company* (Midland, Mich.: Dow Chemical Co., 1978).
5. Eugene Bardach and Lucian Pugliaresi, "The Environmental-Impact Statement vs. The Real World," *Public Interest,* Fall, 1977; "Clearance by EPA for Nuclear Plant Is Voided by Court," *The Wall Street Journal,* February 14, 1978.
6. *Coal Age,* February 1978 and July 1975.
7. Edward F. Denison, "Effects of Selected Changes in the Institu-

tional and Human Environment upon Output per Unit of Input," *Survey of Current Business,* January 1978.

8. Armco Steel Corporation, *1975 Annual Report* (Middletown, Ohio: 1976), p. 3.

9. James F. Ragan, Jr., *Minimum Wages and the Youth Labor Market,* Publication No. 14 (St. Louis: Washington University Center for the Study of American Business, August 1977), pp. 1–12.

10. Robert DeFina, *Public and Private Expenditures for Federal Regulation of Business,* Working Paper No. 22 (St. Louis: Washington University Center for the Study of American Business, 1977).

11. Donald Ubben, "OSHA Noise Standards Stir Debate," *Washington Report,* December 19, 1977.

12. Synfuels Interagency Task Force, *Recommendations for a Synthetic Fuels Commercialization Program,* report submitted to the President's Energy Resources Council, Vol. 1 (Washington, D.C.: GPO, 1975), pp. C-22, 134.

13. F. G. Garibaldi, *Government Procedure and Our Energy Future* (Indianapolis Contemporary Club, 1978), pp. 6–9; correspondence to the author from R. A. Finn, Associate Director of Government and Public Affairs Department, Standard Oil Co. of Ohio, April 26, 1978.

14. "Will EPA Stop Investment?" *First Chicago World Report,* May–June 1978.

15. William D. Carey, "Muddling Through: Government and Technology," *Science,* April 4, 1975.

16. William M. Wardell, "Introduction of New Therapeutic Drugs in the United States and Great Britain: An International Comparison," *Clinical Pharmacology and Therapeutics,* September–October 1973.

17. U. S. Food and Drug Administration, "Trichlorethylene (TCE) and Coffee," *FDA Talk Paper* (Rockville, Md.: U.S.F.D.A., June 27, 1975), p. 1; *Memorandum of Alert: Trichlorethylene,* memorandum from associate director for carcinogenesis, DCCP, NCI to Chairman, DHEW Committee to Coordinate Toxicology and Related Programs, March 21, 1975, p. 1 and attachments; Isadore Barmash, "General Foods Changing Sanka and Brim Solvent," *The New York Times,* July 17, 1975.

18. Ernest B. Hook and Kristine Healy, "Consequences of a Nation-

wide Ban on Spray Adhesives Alleged to Be Human Teratogens and Mutagens," *Science*, February 13, 1976; Comptroller General of the United States, *Banning of Two Toys and Certain Aerosol Spray Adhesives*, MWD-75-65 (Washington, D.C.: U.S. General Accounting Office, 1975), pp. 13–30.

19. W. Paul Zemitzsch, "Pension Reform Law Putting Many Firms in a Quandary," *St. Louis Globe-Democrat*, June 26, 1976; *Industry Week*, August 15, 1977.

3

The Pervasive
Impacts on the
Business Firm

*Old laws and old agencies neither die nor
fade away; being nonbiodegradable, they
only accumulate.*
Bayless Manning
Former Dean, Stanford Law School

IT is hard to overestimate the rapid expansion and the almost
infinite variety of government involvement in business which is
now occurring in the United States. The new type of governmental
regulation of business is not limited to the traditional independent regulatory agencies, such as the Interstate Commerce Commission, the Civil Aeronautics Board, and the Federal Communications Commission. Rather, all the operating bureaus of
government—the Departments of Agriculture, Commerce, Energy, Interior, Justice, Labor, Transportation, Treasury, and
Health, Education, and Welfare—are now involved in actions
that affect virtually every firm in every industry.

Certainly most changes influencing business-government relations in recent years have been in the direction of greater government involvement in many aspects of life: environmental
controls, job safety inspections, equal employment opportunity
enforcement, consumer product safety regulations, and energy

restrictions. Indeed, when we attempt to look at the emerging business–government relationship from the business executive's viewpoint, a very considerable public presence is evident in what historically have been private matters.

No business, large or small, can operate without obeying a myriad of government restrictions and regulations. Costs and profits can be affected as much by a regulation written by a government official as by company moves or customers' changing preferences. The types of management decisions which increasingly are subject to governmental influence, review, or control are fundamental to the business system:

What lines of business to go into?
What products can be produced?
Which investments can be financed?
Under what conditions can products be produced?
Where can products be made?
How can products be marketed?
What prices can be charged?
What profit can be kept?

Like a hall of mirrors in which one's every move is both monitored and mimicked, virtually every major department of the typical corporation in the United States has one or more counterparts in a federal agency that controls or strongly influences its internal decision making:

- The scientists in corporate research laboratories now receive much of their guidance from lawyers in regulatory agencies dealing with various aspects of technological innovation.
- The engineers in manufacturing departments must abide by standards promulgated by Labor Department authorities.
- The sales personnel in marketing organizations must follow procedures established by government administrators in product safety agencies and, to a growing extent, receive advance approval before marketing new products.
- Officials deciding the location of facilities must conform with a variety of environmental statutes.
- Personnel staffs are increasingly restricted by the many ex-

ecutive agencies concerned with one or more aspects of employment conditions.

- The accountants and statisticians in finance departments often bear the brunt of the rising paperwork burden being imposed on business by government agencies.

Because of its complexity and immense size, therefore, it is difficult to grasp the totality of the governmental involvement. But there simply are very few aspects of business activities that escape some type of government review or influence. The impacts of regulation go far beyond general requirements for corporate performance; they increasingly permeate every aspect of consumer activity from the purchase of hair dyes to the installation of swimming pool slides.

In addition to the more obvious types of corporate responses to government intervention discussed in the preceding chapter, a variety of internal adjustments are taking place. Each major corporate function is undergoing an important transformation: reacting to government actions, trying to anticipate or obviate further government activity, or attempting to alter that external environment. The change tends either to increase the overhead costs of business or deflect management and employee attention from the conventional tasks of designing, developing, producing, and distributing new and better or cheaper goods and services.

Bayless Manning, former dean of the Stanford Law School, has pointed out that the increased regulations and new requirements for prior clearance at all levels of government are hobbling the capacity of the economy to make necessary decisions rapidly. Manning refers to private enterprise finding itself "regulated into slow motion." [1] At times it seems that each and every move that business makes is studied with almost obsessive attention by one or more regulatory agencies, far out of proportion to the inherent need for government attention.

TOP MANAGEMENT

The various top management groups are undergoing a fundamental metamorphosis of role as they respond to the changing external environment. Also, the outlook of key corporate executives is shifting from a primary concern with conventional production and marketing decisions to coping with a host of external and often strange policy considerations that frequently are those of groups with nonbusiness and noneconomic priorities. Members of the senior management group may become as attuned to the desires of those new interests as to their traditional accountability to shareholders. As Robert E. Mercer, executive vice president of Goodyear, stated in March 1978 to the Pacific Coast Tire Dealers Association, the tire industry may wind up spending more time dealing with regulation, and thus relegating customer preferences to second place, if present trends of government regulation continue.

The clearest way to see the impacts of regulation on top management is to consider the extent to which management and members of boards of directors are being held more directly accountable for key company policies and activities by various government agencies, notably the Securities and Exchange Commission and the courts. The responsibility for adherence by the entire corporate hierarchy to the mandates of the Food and Drug Administration, the Consumer Product Safety Commission, and other agencies is increasingly being placed personally on the chief executive officer. In one recent landmark case (Acme Markets), the president was fined by a federal court for sanitary violations in one of the company warehouses.

Individual business executives face varying and rising penalties under federal statutes. The maximum individual penalty under the antitrust laws now is a $100,000 fine and three years in jail; the maximum corporate penalty is a $1 million fine and divestiture. Under the Securities Act, the top personal penalty is $10,000 fine and two years in prison; the top corporate punishment is a $10,000 fine and an injunction prohibiting the designated activity. In fiscal 1974, five businessmen spent time in jail under the Sherman Antitrust Act; by 1977, the figure was twenty-three.[2]

It is not surprising that numerous chief executives report that one-third or more of their time is now devoted to government and public policy matters: dealing with the many federal, state, and local regulations that affect the company, meeting with a wide variety of civic and special interest groups that make "demands" on the organization's resources, and increasingly participating in the public policy arena. A survey by The Conference Board revealed that 43 percent of the chief executives responding devote one-fourth or more of their time to external relations and that 92 percent devote more time to that activity than they did three to five years ago.[3]

A type of chief executive very different from that envisioned in popular stereotypes is emerging in American corporations. William Agee, chairman of Bendix Corporation, may have described the emerging outlook of the chief executive of a major corporation in an extreme fashion, but his view surely incorporates a growing aspect of reality:

> Our large corporations have long since ceased to be private institutions, in any meaningful sense of the term. . . . Companies today are accountable not only to their shareholders and their employees but also to what is amorphously called the public, which may mean anything from the Sierra Club to the Federal Trade Commission or a congressional committee.[4]

All in all, then, the "metamorphosis" of the modern corporation at its highest levels is clear: corporate executives are less private entrepreneurs in a free enterprise system than they are unelected "quasi-public officials" in an amorphous and complex system that includes both private and social concerns. Thus, for many people in the business world, the connotation of the word "enterprise" has radically changed from the traditional "innovative, entrepreneurial activity," if, indeed, any of the original connotation remains.

RESEARCH AND DEVELOPMENT

Some of the most fundamental impacts of government intervention are discernible in the corporate research and development area, although the ramifications are likely to become evident only over a long period of time. According to a December 1976 report of the House Committee on Science and Technology, "In most situations, uncertainty in policy and regulatory practices serves as a barrier to innovation. Conflicting regulations constrain industrial R&D."

Scholars are now showing, for example, that recent more stringent regulation by the Food and Drug Administration is a major cause of higher costs, time lags, and rising risk in pharmaceutical innovation. Increased regulation alone accounts for doubling the cost of developing and introducing a new chemical entity in the United States. Jerome E. Schnee, of Rutgers University, has shown in an April 1978 report for the Hoffmann-La Roche pharmaceutical firm that government intervention has had a marked effect on the industry in the last two decades. Prior to 1962—the year in which major amendments to the FDA's authority were enacted—small pharmaceutical firms held their own in R&D. But between 1965 and 1970 the situation changed: the largest drug firms did in fact produce more innovations, relative to their size, than did smaller businesses.

Dr. Schnee points out one other important fact. A 1974 survey of the 15 largest U.S. pharmaceutical companies indicated that, although the firms in the survey did almost no testing abroad in the mid-1960s, the percent of new chemicals first tested abroad increased rapidly after that time. By 1974, one-half of the new chemical entities studied by the 15 firms were first tested outside the United States. Innovation in pharmaceuticals, therefore, has become increasingly concentrated in the large, multinational drug companies, apparently because those firms are better able to bear the additional costs and risks of innovation than smaller companies and also because they can shift their resources from the United States to less regulated countries with similar scientific capabilities.[5]

A similar negative impact on the competitive nature of the American business system is occurring as a result of the new toxic chemical law (the Toxic Substances Control Act, or Tosca). The Environmental Protection Agency itself has said that Tosca may lead to fewer innovative products emerging from the industry and that "small firms may tend to move away from product lines that become targets for Tosca attention." [6]

There is little argument about the general notion that regulation inhibits innovation; the serious disagreements concern degree. Any doubt on that score can be eliminated by recalling the opening policy statement in the Toxic Substances Control Act, in which the Act states that the regulations are intended "not to impede *unduly* or create *unnecessary* economic barriers to technological innovation while fulfilling the primary purpose." [Emphasis added.] It is on those two crucial adjectives, therefore, that the questions and arguments hinge.

Surely the Delaney Amendment to the Food, Drug and Cosmetic Act is a prime example of overkill in health and safety regulation via an implicit zero-risk approach. That statute prohibits the use of any chemical substance in *any* amount as a food additive if the substance has been found, by "appropriate" test, to induce cancer in man or laboratory animals. A major problem becoming increasingly evident in this field of regulation is that scientific progress since the 1950s has brought about a ten-thousand-fold to one-million-fold improvement in the ability to measure "*any* amount." In one case, FDA reported that a suspected substance, DES, was found in animal tissue in the amount of 120 parts per trillion. The report led *The New York Times* to comment editorially (April 30, 1973), "Is there a significant—even an appreciable—risk of anyone getting cancer from meat containing so tiny a quantity of DES? . . . This sounds more like fanaticism than intelligent public policy."

Fortunately for those of us who like (and need) to eat, the Delaney Amendment standards apply only to food additives. But let it be noted that many natural foods contain chemical elements which, in massive doses, can introduce cancer in laboratory animals. Lettuce, for example, contains nickel, a metal which causes cancer and would therefore have to be banned if the criteria of the Delaney Amendment were applied to natural foods. [7] The fact that we do not drop face down in our salad bowls indicates that the human organism must have a tolerance for some level of nickel. *How much,* once again, is the serious but unanswered scientific question, and it is a question which regulatory agencies and their tests have, at least at times, tended wholly to ignore.

The shift away from the type of fundamental research that often yields key product breakthroughs toward more cautious, applied research is already evident among chemical manufacturers. Du Pont, the U.S. chemical industry's leader in research and development spending, has shown a notable retrenchment in its support of R&D over the past few years. In the process, the company has shifted many of its R&D efforts from new-venture research to work on established product lines.[8] Monsanto, another large chemical firm, finds that 13 percent of its research is spent on compliance. It has reorganized its R&D efforts into two parallel organizations; one is the traditional R&D staff, and the new organization is termed the environmental policy staff.[9]

Thus a rising share of corporate R&D budgets is being shifted to so-called defensive research, that is, to meeting the requirements of governmental regulatory agencies, from designing products with greater customer appeal. The trend is most advanced in the automotive industry. In the words of Arjay Miller, former president of the Ford Motor Company and now dean of the Stanford University Graduate School of Business, "There is just so much capacity for change, and the talent and money have been going into safety and emission requirements."

The head of the General Motors research laboratory has used stronger language in describing the situation: "We've diverted a large share of our resources—sometimes up to half—into meeting government regulations instead of developing better materials, better manufacturing techniques, and better products. . . . It's a terrible way to waste your research dollars."[10] On the one hand, of course, we may see such "diversionary" expenditures as excessive reactions to the massively burdensome government regulations. On the other hand, however, some may view defensive research more cautiously and consider it to be not wasteful but merely prudent, at least from the viewpoint of the individual company.

Unfortunately, except for such dramatic cases as the proposed ban on saccharin to be discussed later, the consumer is not likely to feel the impacts of the shift to "defensive research" for many years, when the reversal of the process may be extremely difficult and surely may not be accomplished within a short period of time.

MANUFACTURING

The combined impacts of the rulings of EPA, OSHA, FDA, and CPSC, to cite just the most conspicuous agencies, are altering major aspects of the manufacturing function of the typical American business firm. One result of the pressures for production processes to meet government environmental and safety requirements is that a larger share of company investment—about one-tenth at the present time—is being devoted to the required social responsibilities rather than to increasing the capacity to produce a higher quantity or quality of material output, at least as conventionally measured. Coupled with the many factory closings due to regulation mentioned earlier, the result of the requirements is a smaller productive capacity in the American economy than is generally realized.

It is clear that the governmentally mandated pollution control expenditures have seriously affected the investment process of key industries. For one thing, the very length of the investment process has been prolonged, partly because of the permit applications and partly because of the increased uncertainty engendered by both the unpredictability of future legislation and the case-by-case application of pollution controls. The paper industry has experienced severe delays; 35 percent of its expenditures have been postponed for a period of 15 months or more. The lengthening of the time frame of investment spending caused by pollution control standards represents an important secondary cost on industry through its tendency to lower the rate of capital formation.[11]

In a March 1978 study done for the Environmental Protection Agency, Arthur D. Little, Inc. concluded that environmental regulations will have severe repercussions on the productive capacity of the copper industry. The study showed that existing regulations plus the continuing uncertainty regarding new regulations and the way they will be enforced will undoubtedly slow down domestic smelter capacity expansion and new resource development generally. According to the Little organization's analysis, the pollution control regulations will add about 23 to 39 percent to copper prices. As a result, production will fall about 25 to 33 percent below what it otherwise would be. In addition, there will be an increase in copper imports of more than 8 percent by 1981 over the baseline figure. The resulting effects, therefore, of a single regulation—as it pertains to *one* industry—can be seen to affect many sectors of the American economy.

The combined effect of a lower stock of productive capital coupled with more expensive and elaborate production and review processes can only result in a decline in the ability of the American economy to deliver the rising living standard which has become a hallmark of the private enterprise system. Surely this is another example of the powerful, though unintentional, results of government intervention which does not take adequate account of the full economic consequences.

MARKETING

Virtually every aspect of the marketing function of business is affected by government. According to Professor G. David Hughes of the University of North Carolina, the growing regulations and court decisions explain why many marketing managers spend most of their time dealing with matters related to the federal government. Increasingly, government regulations are restricting the options available to the marketing manager.

Advertising is subject to basic regulation by the Federal Trade Commission, which has been increasingly concerned with misrepresentation by business firms. On occasion, the government mandates what advertising should contain, as well as what it must not contain. Entire industries have been required to document their advertising claims that product X does shave 50 percent closer or that product Y does contain 50 percent fewer calories. The details of product warranties are controlled by the Magnuson-Moss Act of 1975. Package labeling and/or packaging is now regulated by the Federal Trade Commission, the Food and Drug Administration, the Consumer Product Safety Commission, and the Department of Agriculture. Motor vehicle producers must include mileage ratings in advertising; cigarettes must display statements about their probable link to cancer; appliances must be labeled according to energy usage; and processed foods must list ingredients in specified order.

Certainly, many or most of these regulations are intended to advance and, in fact, enforce what the government perceives to be truth, fairness, and knowledgeability about a product. But that is not to say that the regulations themselves, as written and as applied in all their astonishing complexity, always are inherently "good."

For example, one recent action by a regulatory agency, the saccharin warning labeling procedure instituted by the Food and Drug Administration, provides some understanding of the detailed nature of the intervention in the marketing activity. In November 1977 Congress passed the Saccharin Study and Labeling Act. That law was hailed as a victory for the concept of individual consumer choice, because it prohibited FDA for a period of 18 months from banning saccharin from the food supply. The new law, however, also required warning labels on food containing saccharin and mandated that posters be placed in retail stores that sell such food.

The FDA seems to have had a field day in writing the regulations implementing the Act. For example, the regulations require that the warning must appear in a conspicuous place on the label of the product, usually on each principal display panel, in easily readable boldface type with each letter at least one-sixteenth of an inch high. Generally, the warning must appear immediately above or below the product name. The FDA also tells the retail stores how they must warn customers about foods with saccharin in them. Stores selling such foods must post notices at least 11 by 14 inches in size, on white card stock, and in gothic type. The background of the heading and the warning statement are required to be bright red with white lettering. In the case of any retail store over 10,000 square feet, the notices should be posted in three places: near the store's entrance, in the area where the greatest quantity of diet soft drinks are sold, and in the area where the largest amount of other saccharin-containing food is displayed.

Retail establishments of more than 3,200 square feet but less than 10,000 square feet must display at least two notices. Stores of less than 3,200 square feet must display at least one notice. The exact language of the notice is specified by the FDA:

> SACCHARIN NOTICE. This store sells food including diet beverages and dietetic food that contain saccharin. You will find saccharin listed in the ingredient statement on most foods which contain it. All foods which contain saccharin will soon bear the following warning: "Use of this product may be hazardous to your health. This product contains saccharin, which has been determined to cause cancer in laboratory animals." This store is required by law to display this notice prominently.

The FDA has issued a further guideline for displaying the saccharin warning on vending machines, but those extensive details need not be recited here.[12] With a little imagination we may sketch a picture of a food package of the future: a large economy size can or box with enough space for all of the warning, nutritional, and use information increasingly dictated by federal agencies—and barely room for the brand name.

It takes but little thought to recognize that all those detailed procedures required in the case of a single substance, saccharin, are time-consuming and costly to implement. Moreover, it takes only a small addition of thought to recognize that the regulations are only *temporary:* even more detailed and more costly procedures may be set down in future regulations (pending more, and costly, government reviews, of course).

Marketing departments are increasingly responsible for "reverse distribution" in the form of product recalls, including those required by such government agencies as the Consumer Product Safety Commission. That in turn often necessitates a major expansion in record keeping so the holders of the recalled products, final purchasers as well as wholesale and retail distributors, can be promptly notified and so that the required information can be furnished to the appropriate government agency. The paperwork burden—costly in and of itself and part of the snowball effect of regulation we have noticed before—increases by quantum leaps as the number of products, consumers, and pieces of regulatory legislation rises year after year.

As Professors Jules Backman and John Czepiel have written,

> Clearly, today's marketing strategist must be a broken field runner, traversing the field between what his organization can do and is interested in doing, that which the consumer needs and wants, and that which society collectively allows and requires him to do.[13]

Businesses thus are pressured into further "diversionary" expenditures that are caused when they must turn their attention—their *divided* attention—to considerations influenced and complicated by the society of which they are a part and the government to which they are becoming increasingly accountable.

PERSONNEL

At times it seems that the primary thrust of many personnel departments has shifted from serving the staffing needs of the company to meeting the requirements of and pressures from government agencies. Certainly, keeping the company "out of trouble" and avoiding the publicity attendant on charges of discrimination have become no little achievements. In general, a company can get into trouble with government agencies if it asks an applicant questions that indicate—directly or indirectly—any preference or discriminatory ideas about race, religion, color, national origin, sex, age, disability, or marital status. The following are a dozen examples of such questions that usually are off limits:

What is your complexion?
What is your mother tongue?
Are you married?
Where does your spouse work?
What are the ages of your children, if any?
How old are you?

Do you have a disability?
Have you ever been treated for any of the following diseases?
Have you ever worked under another name? Is so, state name
and dates.
Where were you born?
Of what country are you a citizen?
Have you ever been arrested?

In that regard a company may on occasion find itself in a no-win situation. One that did was the Bank of America, which in 1974 settled two class action sex discrimination suits by setting up a $3.8 million trust fund "to provide more banking leadership to help solve the problem of equal opportunity for women." As it turned out, the expenditures from the trust fund did little either to improve the public image of the bank or to demonstrate or promote female banking leadership. One woman received $2,500 to tour the wine-producing regions of Europe and attend a cooking course in Paris; another got $2,500 to visit Ethiopia, Kenya, and Tanzania. Unsurprisingly, the federal court terminated the trust fund one year after its establishment.

The major regulatory agencies active in the personnel area can be cataloged as follows:

• The Equal Employment Opportunity Commission investigates and rules on charges of discrimination. It requires government contractors to develop affirmative-action programs affecting hiring, training, promoting, and terminating the employment status of workers. Affirmative action has been extended in recent years to cover race, sex, veterans, and handicapped personnel.

• Contested OSHA enforcement actions are subject to review by the Occupational Safety and Health Review Commission.

• The Department of Labor's Employment Standards Administration sets and administers standards under laws relating to minimum wages, overtime, and so on. Congress raised the minimum wage again in late 1977.

• The National Labor Relations Board conducts union representation elections and regulates labor practices of employers and unions. Congress is considering Carter administration proposals to toughen penalties on employers running afoul of the Board's rulings.

• Union representation elections in the railroad and airline industries are conducted by the National Mediation Board, which also mediates labor-management disputes.

• The Department of Labor (Labor Management Services Administration) and Department of the Treasury (Internal Revenue Service) jointly determine eligibility of employee welfare and pension plans and set standards for financial disclosure. The Pension Benefit Guaranty Corporation rules on adequacy of assets prior to termination of such plans; it may start termination proceedings on its own.

• Under 1973 legislation, companies employing 25 people or more must offer their employees membership in a health maintenance organization, if a qualified one is available, as an alternative to the company's conventional medical insurance plan. The Department of Health, Education, and Welfare sets the rules for qualification.

Some indication of the almost infinite variation in regulatory procedures that companies must follow is contained in the various requirements for posting information for employees. The following is a partial tabulation.[14]

Category of Company	*Type of Required Poster*
All employers engaged in interstate commerce	Fair Labor Standards Act (regulating wages and hours)
All employers in industries affecting interstate commerce	Occupational safety and health
Employers of 11 or more	Annual summary OSHA form 2 (posted only in February)
Employers of 15 or more and government contractors and subcontractors regardless of size	Equal employment opportunity

Category of Company	*Type of Required Poster*
Employers of 20 or more who are engaged in interstate commerce	Age discrimination
Government contractors and subcontractors with contracts over $2,500	Prohibition of discrimination against the handicapped
Employers directly involved in providing more than $10,000 worth of government-contracted goods and services	Walsh-Healy Public Contracts Act
Construction contractors for federally financed construction	Davis-Bacon Public Contracts Act (setting "prevailing" wages)

FINANCE

To an increasing extent, corporate finance departments are reacting to external demands for information, rather than merely meeting the corporation's own data requirements for internal planning, reporting, and control. That may not be too subtle an indication of the shifting of the locus of corporate decision making from entirely within the firm to an environment in which a variety of other organizations and considerations figure actively.

To begin with, a battery of financial information on company operations is being required by the Securities and Exchange Commission. In addition to requirements to be met before issuing stocks and bonds, the SEC has mandated far more detail in corporate annual reports than has been traditionally released. Likewise, financial transactions of commercial banks and their customers are subject to expanding regulation by the Federal Reserve System, the Federal Deposit Insurance Corporation, and the Comptroller of the Currency, via the truth-in-lending law of 1968 and more recent enactments dealing with credit discrimination against women, and so on.

The government's demand for information drives businesses

into a blizzard of paper and red tape, as we have seen in Chapter 2. In the aggregate, the Federal Paperwork Commission recently estimated that the total cost of federal paperwork imposed on private industry ranges from $25 to $32 billion a year and that "a substantial portion of this cost is unnecessary." Unfortunately, the drive for increased corporate "openness" appears to be based on the notion that more is always better than less and that information is a free good. The consequence of "openness" may simply be onerousness.

The current disclosure fad is likely to engender all sorts of adverse, though unintended, effects. The chief executive officer of one major California bank reports that disclosure for disclosure's sake of detailed and often private material not only is irrelevant and confusing but also causes many small and medium-size companies to be excluded from the capital markets by the formidable and complex disclosure requirements of the SEC.[15] That, of course, has anticompetitive results simply because it reduces the ability of small companies to develop and expand.

FACILITIES

Company factories, warehouses, offices, and other facilities must meet increasingly rigorous standards on environmental quality set by the Environmental Protection Agency and the state, county, and municipal counterparts. Also, individual industries are often subject to specialized regulations, and it is not uncommon for their regulators to disagree. Nuclear facilities, for example, are subject to detailed regulation by the Nuclear Regulatory Commission (NRC), but the construction of the cooling towers has to be approved by the Federal Aviation Administration. Acceptable impact statements must be prepared for a variety of environmental agencies, and numerous other state and local regulatory requirements must be met.

A former chairman of the NRC has described vividly the process of what he calls "regulatory shuttlecock" between federal agencies, whereby construction of an electric power plant in New Hampshire was halted for more than half a year after it had been authorized. He lamented that large numbers of government agencies have the uncoordinated power to say no to a proposed electric generating facility, whether nuclear or fossil, but no single body can give a definitive yes.[16] The NRC itself commented on the situation in unusually strong terms for a government agency: "a system strangling itself and the economy in red tape." The agency has put some price tags on the effect of the red tape. It estimates that costs for delay in starting construction on a new power plant average over $9 million a month. The cost of delay in starting operations after a plant has been built range between $8.5 and $13 million a month. Such are the tremendous costs in only *one* instance of government's regulatory spiderwebbing.

It is ironic to note that many of the existing federal, state, and local regulatory policies tend to discourage companies from taking the "socially responsible" route of locating manufacturing operations in central cities. The policies which generally favor rural or suburban areas include zoning, noise limitations, and environmental restrictions on air and water use. As the Campbell Soup Company wrote (in November 1977) in response to an inquiry on the subject by the Banking and Housing Committee of the U.S. House of Representatives, rural locations generally make it easier to minimize any adverse effects a facility may have on the local environment and to meet or surpass any government environmental requirements, all at considerably less cost than in the city. An irony such as that shows us how so much of our national life is caught up, unwittingly, in the regulatory web.

STAFF OPERATIONS

Expansions in selected staff operations often constitute the most direct company response to the widening role of government in business. Virtually every company is developing some capability to inform itself about and evaluate present and future government developments as they relate to its activities. Firms of substantial size generally maintain headquarters planning staffs and Washington offices, whereas smaller companies rely primarily on their trade associations and on Washington-based attorneys and consultants. In some cases, more substantial changes are made in the corporate organizational structure. A company may establish a major headquarters office on government relations with direct ties to each of its operating departments.

One of the greatest corporate changes has been that of business dealings with the law and the courts. Dow Chemical's public relations manager, Jim Hansen, states, "Any company will tell you its fastest-growing department is its legal department, and its legal department is dealing mainly in regulatory matters." Dow maintains a Washington staff of 20 specialists to keep it informed of the various activities of federal departments and agencies. In the same fashion, New York's Citibank, the nation's second largest financial institution, reported in August 1977 that its domestic legal bill exceeds the total earnings of the great majority of banks in the United States.

A related development is the expansion of corporate public relations or public affairs functions to include basic questions of public policy affecting the American business system. Existing channels of communication—ranging from employee newspapers to customer magazines to annual reports to shareholders—are increasingly utilized to raise the public consciousness on key issues affecting the company and the business system generally.

INDUSTRY STRUCTURE

Government regulation, often unwittingly, hits small business disproportionately hard. Most of the impact is unintentional, in that the standardized regulations typically do not distinguish among companies of different sizes. But in practice, forcing a very small firm to fill out the same specialized forms as a large company with highly trained technical staffs at its disposal places a significantly greater burden on the smaller enterprise. That general point is supported by data and examples from such different government regulatory activities as the Environmental Protection Agency, the Employee Retirement Income Security Act, the

National Labor Relations Board, the Occupational Safety and Health Administration, and the Securities and Exchange Commission.

Smaller companies are likely to be most adversely affected by across-the-board regulatory activity, and they experience even more difficulty surviving as independent entities. A few examples will emphasize the point. In the late 1960s the foundry industry began to lose small plants, those that specialized in small orders of less than 500 pieces a year, because of a combination of economic recession and government regulation. The castings produced by the foundries are critical for production of small runs of capital equipment. But the cost of the mandated EPA emission control expenditures for many of the foundries that closed exceeded the net worth of the entire operation.[17] The larger foundries generally were able to absorb the added government-mandated costs—and ultimately to pass them on to their customers in the form of higher prices.

The proposed OSHA standards for air lead exposure levels furnish another example of a small business that is adversely affected. Charles River Associates, a consulting firm, estimates that the cost to the battery industry of initial compliance would be approximately $416 million (in 1976 dollars) and the continuing costs would be $112 million a year.[18] The lead regulations would result in much larger per unit production costs for smaller plants than for larger plants. Because of large differential costs and the fact that battery prices would tend to rise to cover the unit costs of the larger firms, the consulting firm concluded that smaller operators would be forced to absorb the cost differential. In many cases the amount absorbed would eliminate entirely the plant's profitability, and about 113 single-plant battery firms would be forced to close. The prospective closures would eliminate half of the productive capacity not operated by the five major battery companies.

In sum, the examples show the strong and potentially destructive power which government regulation can wield over small businesses. That power has obvious repercussions not only on small businesses but also on the overall structure of the American economy.

In specific ways, some government regulations adversely affect the ability of small enterprises to attract investment. The "prudent man" rules included in ERISA (the pension reform law), coupled with their accent on personal liability for the "imprudent" pension fund manager, have accentuated the trend to concentrate equity investments in the larger, well-established companies. Some of the Securities and Exchange Commission's rules also tend to work against small firms. The SEC definition of a "private offering" is the solicitation of no more than 25 potential investors and sale of stock to no more than 10 investors. SEC registration for "public offerings" may cost between $100,000 and $150,000 to prepare, and can take four to six months.[19]

It is much more difficult, on the other hand, to assess the impact of regulations that are merely burdensome to small business, such as meeting the paperwork requirements. The Commission on Federal Paperwork reported that 5 million small businesses spend from $15 to $20 billion a year, or an average of over $3,000 each, on federal paperwork. As the Commission pointed out, small businesses are relatively harder hit by federal information requirements than larger firms and often lack the necessary expertise to comply.

What may not be apparent to most people is the basically anti-competitive nature of the regulations of federal agencies. As we have seen, the problems being faced by the larger companies should not be underestimated, but it is realistic to expect that most of the larger companies will be able to adjust to and survive in the expanded regulatory environment, although at higher levels of cost and reduced rates of output. Surely it is not the intent of the groups that favor expanding the role of government to single out the smaller firm. In fact, those interest groups typically focus their criticism on the giants of industry. Ironically, the result is often the reverse of what was intended—a weakening of the role which small and new firms play in the American economy and a more concentrated industrial structure.

SUMMARY

We have tried to take a broad overview of the wide range and variety of government intervention in business decision making and to assess the influence of that intervention. It is not difficult to see that both the nature of government actions and the effects the actions have on business are pervasive and can often hobble business efficiency.

Certainly that is not to say that government intervention, in and of itself, is evil and that it should be eliminated. But the massive exercise of government power raises these key questions: Do its advantages in a given instance outweigh its disadvantages? Do its ends (both economic and social) justify either its means or its unplanned side effects?

Few, if any, sectors of the economy go untouched by public intervention. Complex interrelations abound in the regulatory labyrinth—conflicting regulations among the agencies themselves and ripple effects of regulation throughout the private sector. Moreover, as we have seen, business-government relations in the United States in recent years have been far from a static affair. In fact, there are numerous indications that the developments that we have been analyzing are accelerating.

References

1. Bayless Manning, "Hyperlexis: Our National Disease," *Northwestern University Law Review*, January–February 1977.
2. David Burnham, "Tougher Penalties in Antitrust Cases," *The New York Times*, March 16, 1978; *Business Week*, May 10, 1976.
3. Phyllis S. McGrath, *Managing Corporate External Relations* (New York: The Conference Board, 1976), p. 49.
4. William M. Agee, "The Moral and Ethical Climate in Today's Business World," *MSU Business Topics*, Winter 1978.
5. Henry G. Grabowski and John M. Vernon, "Consumer Protection in Ethical Drugs," *American Economic Review*, February 1977.

6. "EPA Assailed on Toxic Substances Plans," *Chemical and Engineering News*, March 21, 1977.
7. *Monsanto Speaks Up About Chemicals* (St. Louis: Monsanto Co., 1977), p. 7.
8. "Du Pont Shifts R&D Toward Established Lines," *Chemical and Engineering News*, October 3, 1977.
9. "Government Regulatory Costs: Getting Out of Hand?" *Chemical Week*, August 10, 1977.
10. "How GM Manages Its Billion-Dollar R&D Program," *Business Week*, June 28, 1976.
11. David Condon, "Pollution Control Legislation and the Capital Appropriations/Expenditure Lag," *Monthly Review of the Federal Reserve Bank of San Francisco*, March 1978.
12. "Saccharin Warning Allowed on Closures by FDA; Vending Rules Proposed," *NSDA Bulletin*, February 27, 1978.
13. Jules Backman and John Czepiel, "Marketing Strategy: Some Basic Considerations," in Jules Backman and John Czepiel, eds., *Changing Marketing Strategies in a New Economy* (Indianapolis: Bobbs-Merrill, 1977), p. 19.
14. "Required Government Posters," *Boardroom Reports*, July 30, 1978.
15. Thomas R. Wilcox, "Developing Marketing Strategies in Financial Institutions," in Backman and Czepiel, op. cit., p. 126.
16. Marcus A. Rowden, "Licensing of Nuclear Power Plants," *Regulation*, January–February 1978.
17. Kenneth W. Chilton, *The Impact of Federal Regulation on American Small Business* (St. Louis: Washington University Center for the Study of American Business, 1978).
18. "CRA Examines the Costs of Meeting OSHA Lead Standards," *Charles River Associates Research Review*, February 1978.
19. "ERISA 'Hurting' Small Firms," *St. Louis Post-Dispatch*, June 24, 1977.

4

The Shape of Things to Come: An Optimistic Perspective

The government is assuming the role of the silent partner who no longer wishes to remain silent.
Douglas Lambert and James Stock
MSU Business Topics

THE present trends in government regulation of business in the United States are not an abrupt departure from an idealized free market economy. Rather, they are a rapid intensification of the long-term expansion of government influence over the private sector. Some historical perspective is useful in evaluating the prospects for future change in business-government relations.

THE HISTORICAL CONTEXT

The Comptroller of the Currency, for example, has been licensing national banks since 1863. The Interstate Commerce Commission began to regulate railroad rates and routes in 1887. The Antitrust Division of the Department of Justice was set up in 1903 to prosecute violators of the Sherman Antitrust Act, and the Federal Trade Commission was given authority to promote competitive behavior under the Clayton Act of 1914. A host of regulatory agencies was established in the 1930s, a period of rapid and almost overwhelming national change: the Securities and Exchange Commission, the Federal Deposit Insurance Corporation, the Federal Home Loan Bank Board, the Federal Power Commission, the Civil Aeronautics Board, the Federal Maritime Commission, the Federal Communications Commission, the Food and Drug Administration, the Animal and Plant Health Inspection Service, and the National Labor Relations Board.

Each of those regulatory agencies had an important impact on some part of the economy, and each continues to have one. But in the main, the agencies were limited to specific industries (for example, railroads or banking) and dealt with a few economic issues (prices to be charged or areas to be served). Those government interventions in the economy constituted a rather specialized affair unrelated to the day-to-day operations of most businesses. In striking contrast, the regulatory agencies established in more recent years are having a more pervasive impact on the business system. The newer agencies increasingly are involved in the day-to-day functioning of all business firms; they affect both the conditions under which goods and services are produced and the basic characteristics of the products that are made.

It is important to understand the changing motivations for government regulatory activity. In the case of the older agencies, the public concern has been mainly that of protecting the consumer against monopoly power. The Antitrust Division and the Federal Trade Commission, in their different ways, try to eliminate corporate activities that diminish the effectiveness of market competition. The Interstate Commerce Commission, the Civil Aeronautics Board, the Federal Communications Commission, and the banking agencies serve the dual function of controlling the access of new firms into a given industry (via their power to grant franchises or licenses) and regulating various aspects of the economic function of those firms, especially their prices. In the absence of competition, government regulation has been utilized in those two instances to provide the counterpart of what would be the competitive market in an effort to protect the consumer as well as the shareholder.

The major interest groups involved are "producers" of various sorts, such as farmers, manufacturers, and commercial firms. Frequently, the companies in the regulated industry and the unions representing their employees have become the most vocal supporters of the regulatory apparatus to which they are subject. But the pressures for the expansion of the newest types of regulation have been mainly noneconomic. This time the key interest groups include environmental organizations, civil rights groups, and consumer organizations, all representing important social rather than primarily economic approaches to public policy.

The relatively recent and more vocal concern with the impacts of business activities on the physical environment led to the establishment of the Environmental Protection Agency in 1970. Reduction of hazards to consumers motivated the establishment in 1972 of the Consumer Product Safety Commission. Worker safety and health were the reasons for the introduction of the Occupational Safety and Health Administration in 1973. As we have seen in the preceding chapters, the newer agencies influence virtually all aspects of business decision making and affect management at all levels—line and staff, top and middle management, and also first-line supervisors.

Thus the latest shifts in national values, although previously noneconomic in their motivation, have had and continue to have important economic ramifications. The shifts have included less concern with economic growth and employment and more emphasis on equity and the quality of life both on and off the job.

The substantial dissatisfaction with the results of business performance surely is visible nationwide, whether we look at the daily paper or at the reports of public opinion polls. Recent polls have produced some disturbing data on what people believe about American business and the private enterprise system. When the Louis Harris Survey measured public confidence levels in the leadership of most American institutions in April 1975, it found that only 19 percent of those polled had "a great deal of confidence" in the major U.S. companies. That represented a substantial decline of public esteem for business from the 1966 level of 55 percent.[1] Similarly, the Gallup Poll, in June 1976, stated that "evidence of an anti-business mood in the country is seen in the findings which show business executives to be far down the list" in ratings of ethical standards for professions. Business ranked below doctors, engineers, and college teachers and just above labor union leaders.[2]

More recently, in January 1977, the Gallup Poll reported a doubling over the last decade in the percent of people saying the country has most to fear from big business (although big government still ranked highest as the perceived threat). The same poll showed that only about half of the people surveyed had any strong confidence in the American economic system of free enterprise.[3]

Dissatisfaction with business performance in part reflects a shift in the ground rules of what is expected of the business system, as well as a widespread belief that business has a major responsibility for many of the social problems facing society. The point made here is not that the dissatisfactions necessarily have a factual base or are fully justified. Rather, the key point is that the dissatisfactions with the business system do *exist*; and as long as they continue, they are likely to cause further expansions of government power over business decision making.

What the extent of government regulation will be in the years ahead is, of course, an open question. One of the few things we can count on, though, is that, if the trend of the last two decades persists, the sheer number of regulations annually poured into the Federal Register will continue to increase by the thousands. The regulatory apparatus may become for American business an ever more elaborate and confusing maze of rules and restrictions. At the same time, however, it is important to understand the nature of pressures which motivate the rapid expansion of regulatory activity, pressures which are likely to continue: protecting employees from discrimination and health risks, protecting customers from severe product hazards, and protecting the interests of all citizens in the conservation of natural resources and the health of the physical environment. Those concerns certainly are obvious and important to us all, but the concerns themselves are not, in the last analysis, what is at issue in this book.

There is no intention here to question what the nature of government intervention should be or the effectiveness and reasonableness of specific regulatory activities. But it may be helpful to understand that the differences among the wide range of interest groups, strong as they may be, mainly relate to the means used to achieve the objectives rather than the merits of the ends, the desirable goals. As a nation, we want to improve the quality of life of our citizens, but it should be self-evident that to state a worthy end is not to justify *any* means of achieving it.

It may be useful at this point to examine the major possibilities for change in business-government relations in the United States during the coming decade. Two fundamentally different approaches for change are being urged on government policy makers. One is to seek improvement in business-government relations by reforming the existing array of government regulatory and ancillary undertakings. The other is to deal with the continuing shortcomings of and dissatisfactions with the business system by further government involvement in economic activity.

To be sure, a third approach is present, the desire to return to a simpler age with limited government involvement in private affairs. This book will give little attention to that alternative, not so much because of philosophical disagreement, but rather because a return to the status quo ante is not a reasonable expectation. However, it must be acknowledged that successful pursuit of the first approach—reform of what already exists—might well result in a streamlined regulatory system, one that is both smaller and more effective than that which we presently have. That approach is the subject of the remainder of this chapter. The following chapter is devoted to the second approach: further government involvement in business affairs.

The first approach, incremental reform, is a relatively modest one. It takes into account that existing government regulation is an extremely vast and ambitious undertaking. Therefore, incremental reform is mainly concerned with the serious shortcomings of existing government intervention in economic activity. It stresses opportunities for correction and improvement; it means accepting, by and large, the current division of public and private economic responsibilities but with some opportunity for reducing the proliferation of government activities.

Maintaining the status quo in government policy would not, however, by itself result in any significant lessening in the growth rate of government activity. In July 1978 the U.S. Council on Wage and Price Stability estimated that a portion of the rules then pending in federal agencies could increase consumer and business costs by $35 billion a year. In addition, business would have to invest an additional $60 billion in government-mandated capital equipment—all on the basis of existing legislation.[4] Clearly, legislated reforms would be necessary to change the upward trend of government intervention.

PROSPECTS FOR DEREGULATION

Several key proposals for reform of the present framework of business-government relations have been made. The first relates to the older regulatory commissions, each of which has jurisdiction over one industry or a few related industries such as the Interstate Commerce Commission's regulation of railroads and trucking and the Civil Aeronautics Board's regulation of airlines. Here is where the issue of deregulation—dismantling or at least substantially cutting back the scope of government intervention—has been raised. Both the Ford and Carter administrations have urged Congress to reduce the degree of regulation by the Interstate Commerce Commission and the Civil Aeronautics Board by permitting some competition on prices charged and routes served.

In those cases, greater dependence on competitive market forces can be an effective alternative to detailed government oversight. That is the view of many economists, who maintain that the traditional type of regulation constitutes a form of protection for the existing firms in an industry and serves as a barrier to the entry of new firms. Entrenched firms are thus shielded from potential new competition. That explains, at least in part, why regulatory reform is often opposed by both business and labor groups in the traditionally regulated industries.

In numerous instances the ICC has denied even temporary authority to new companies although existing, authorized truckers were unable or unwilling to meet the needs of shippers. A company that ships fresh meat needed specialized trailers for the purpose. Even though it lacked the equipment, the trucker who already had ICC's authorization to provide the service successfully opposed an application by a trucker who had the equipment and whom the shipper wanted to use!

Truckers that are authorized by the ICC often play what is called the protest game. They automatically file a protest to each and every application by another company which might infringe in any way on their authority, with no regard for either their ability to meet the shipper's needs or their interest in the particular traffic involved. Those protests are frequently boiler plate—they use the same language in each case. The General Accounting Office—the congressional watchdog over federal agencies—reports instances when the protests were so boiler plate that they did not even mention the willingness or ability of the authorized shipper to provide the service—items which, according to the ICC's *Field Staff Manual,* are to be included in each protest.[5]

Clearly, the traditional form of regulation often confers arbitrary benefits on a small number of companies and their employees—to the detriment of the business system and most especially the consuming public. In such instances, deregulation is a most appropriate policy option.

BENEFIT/COST ANALYSIS

The newer forms of regulation constitute a varied lot; in general, they deal with the external public impacts of ostensibly private actions. In the case of environmental protection, for example, there is widespread although not universal agreement that the social costs of pollution warrant government intervention in private economic activity. However, there is considerable disagreement as to the most effective methods to use. Many economists prefer working through the price system rather than relying on detailed standards and specific regulations.

In the case of the newer types of regulatory activity that affect all industry—such as job health or product safety—benefit/cost analysis is a useful way to reconcile a variety of conflicting attitudes and viewpoints. Benefit/cost analysis literally requires regulatory agencies to estimate the total costs of the regulations they promulgate (including what we have seen are the heavy compliance expenses in the private sector) as well as the total benefits that the nation is likely to achieve from the government action. Benefit/cost analysis is a neutral concept; the same weight is given to a dollar of costs as to a dollar of benefit. There is no advance assurance that a benefit/cost analysis will support a given regulation or that it will condemn it. But if it is properly conceived and carefully executed, the benefit/cost approach will go a long way toward insuring that the government's regulatory decision-making process will encompass far more effects than traditionally has been the case.

In the case discussed earlier, in which OSHA proposed to reduce noise in the workplace, benefit/cost analysis could have revealed that wearing ear protectors was a far more economical approach than the alternative of engineering the noise out of the environment.

Other examples of informational shortcomings in the existing approach to regulatory legislation are not hard to find. For example, New York City consumer organizations did not know that they were eliminating the only biodegradable meat tray from their market when they successfully lobbied for a law requiring 100 percent visibility in meat packaging. Moreover, the new containers do not in practice always provide complete visibility because, unlike the packaging they replaced, they do not soak up the blood that may drip out of the product.[6]

A properly applied benefit/cost test is a way to measure objectively the important impacts—good and bad, direct and indirect—that flow from a government regulatory program. Likewise, however, the shortcomings of benefit/cost analysis must be recognized, and also overcome. A government agency (or any other organization) has a natural tendency to be generous in estimating the good that it does and to deprecate the magnitude of the resources required to achieve that good. Such administrative changes as providing ground rules for the analysis developed by an agency with no stake in regulatory activity—the General Accounting Office or the Office of Management and Budget, for example—can minimize but not eliminate those problems.

The fundamental good of the benefit/cost approach is to encourage government officials to take account of the costs as well as the benefits and, more broadly, of the disadvantages as well as the advantages of their actions—and to do so from the viewpoint of society as a whole. Benefit/cost analysis surely is no green-eyeshade approach, oblivious to the real needs of people. The role of the approach was clearly and accurately conveyed by Merril Eisenbud, director of New York University's Laboratory for Environmental Studies and New York City's first environmental administrator: "We aren't keeping an eye on what is truly important—the health and well-being of people—and on cost-benefit ratios—how much we can improve health with a given expenditure of money resources." [7] As a prime example of a misplaced priority, Dr. Eisenbud cites the expenditure of $200 million a year to reduce the level of sulfur in fuel burned in New York City from 0.6 to 0.3 percent. Although he fully supports control over sulfur dioxide emissions into the air, which can cause respiratory problems, he says there is no evidence that the 0.3 percent standard set by the government in what he calls "an excess of zeal" is any better for health. He urges that the $200 million be used more productively.

One can speculate about the improved government decision making that would result from regulatory benefit/cost analysis. Grain elevators are an example of potential application. An average of 13 major explosions of grain elevators occurred in the

United States each year during the period 1976–1978, a rise from an annual average of 8 earlier. It turns out that the frequency of explosions rose following an EPA ruling that prevented the companies from allowing grain dust to escape into the atmosphere. The retained grain dust becomes extremely explosive.[8] EPA clearly did not take account of the total cost of their regulation—especially the lives lost in grain elevator explosions.

Another approach to difficult problems is cost-effectiveness analysis. It is a methodology that can be used when benefits cannot be assigned a dollar value, as in the perennial question of the value of a human life. A given level of achievement is attempted. Obviously, our resources are not infinite, and that must be acknowledged in, for example, attempting to identify the most effective way to reduce automobile accidents by x percent. Essentially the search is for least-cost solutions to policy problems, rather than a trade-off of dollars for lives. In practice, however, public policy frequently does trade off dollars (or consumer convenience) for lives. A 55-miles-per-hour speed limit has lowered the highway accident rate; a 45-mph speed limit probably would reduce the driving toll even further, but it is beyond likely public acceptance. Similarly, restricting airplane landings at each airfield to one every 15 minutes probably would reduce airway accidents, but at unacceptable cost and inconvenience to air travelers.

An economist's viewpoint is that government regulation should be carried to the point where the added benefits equal the added costs, and no further. (Indeed, that is the basic criterion which is generally used to screen proposed government investments in physical resources.) Overregulation—which can be defined as situations in which the costs exceed the benefits—would be avoided. But if policy makers are allowed to ignore or downplay the costs, they are bound to operate in the zone of overregulation, which is where we are today.

An important first step to implement the cost-effectiveness approach—limiting costs to benefits obtained—is that of the inflation impact statements initiated under the Ford administration and retitled economic impact statements. The program has been continued by President Carter. Although the statements are no panacea, the very act of preparing them is encouraging some of the regulatory agencies to broaden their traditional ways of proceeding.[9] The requirement does force government policy makers and administrators to consider the various effects of their actions before the actions are undertaken. But important shortcomings remain. For example, there is no legal requirement that the regulatory agencies give the economic analysis any special weight in their decision making even if the data show that the costs will exceed the benefits.

Through legislation, Congress could put teeth into the required economic impact statements. Forcing an unsympathetic regulator merely to perform some economic analysis may serve little purpose beyond delaying the regulatory process and making it more costly. But limiting government regulation to instances in which the total benefits to society exceed the costs—which should be the heart of any economic impact statement—would be a major and highly desirable departure from current practice. In any event, the overriding point is that the various advantages and disadvantages of a proposed government action should be evaluated before the action is taken.

Unfortunately, the most recent trend in federal regulation seems to be in the opposite direction: single-minded concentration on eliminating every possible hazard no matter how remote or how small the resultant benefit. In the summer of 1978, OSHA held hearings on its general carcinogen proposal. The proposed regulation assumes that there is no safe level of exposure to any carcinogen. It would mandate "lowest feasible exposure," but it would do so without adequately considering costs or the effects of the product bans. In fact, OSHA initially refused to evaluate the economic effects of the standards, even though each federal agency is supposed to do so for regulations likely to cost more than $100 million. (It later relented after protests.) Also, OSHA does not provide for performing analyses which might show that there are no observable adverse effects from low-level usage of some of the questioned substances. Hence, in some cases there may be a sensible and acceptable level of exposure. Means of achieving that level of risk could be set on the basis of risk/benefit analysis. However, that broader view will not prevail unless fundamental reforms are made in the current approach to government regulation.

SUNSET LAWS AND BUDGET REVIEW

Several states, notably Colorado, have passed so-called sunset laws which provide that the legislative authority for each government program should expire after a stated period of time. The idea is to develop a mechanism whereby the legislature periodically reviews the justification for each government activity to determine whether the activity is worthwhile to continue in its present form. Bills have been introduced in Congress to apply the sunset approach to regulatory activities.[10]

That would seem to be a worthwhile approach. Many government programs, regulatory and other, tend to prolong their existence far beyond their initial need and justification. In a world of limited resources, the only sensible way to make room for new priorities is periodically to cut back or eliminate older, superseded priorities. In the case of the older, one-industry regulatory agencies, such as the Civil Aeronautics Board, the sunset mechanism could be an effective way to pursue a deregulation strategy.

Although numerous shortcomings of federal regulation result from the way the statutes are administered, many of the fundamental problems in the regulatory area can be traced back to the legislation enacted—the maze of overlapping, conflicting, and excessive regulation. Therefore, legislative changes are a key part of any serious regulatory reform effort, but much attention in the administration of those activities is also warranted.

Because the requested appropriations for the regulatory agencies are relatively small portions of the government's budget, limited attention has been given to the agencies in the budget preparation and review process. But in view of the large costs that the regulatory agencies impose on the U.S. public, the appropriation requests deserve far more attention than they are now getting. One possibility for making the agencies and their budget reviewers more sensitive to the costs imposed on the public is for Congress to give the agencies ostensible "budgets" of private costs that can be incurred by complying with their regulations. An agency would be given not only a budget of $x million for operating costs but also a ceiling of $y billion of social costs that could be imposed during the fiscal period.

As a start, it would be helpful to include in the federal budget a section on the costs of government regulation similar to the existing special analyses on such other extrabudgetary activities as "federal credit programs" (for example, the Export-Import Bank) and "tax expenditures" (for example, the cost of tax loopholes). Such a special analysis would be an initial step toward incorporating total regulatory costs into the federal government's annual budgetary and program review mechanism and coaxing the annual budget process to focus more directly on regulatory activities.

CHANGES IN APPROACH TO REGULATION

Legislative and administrative changes in regulation are clearly important factors, but in a more fundamental way it is attitudes that would have to be changed in order to have a more effective regulatory system. The experience gained by both government and business under the job safety program provides a case in point. Although the government's safety requirements have resulted in billions of dollars in public and private outlays, very little progress has actually been made toward the goal of a safer work environment. The economist's complaint here, as in other instances, is not the high cost of government regulation—and it is indeed high—but the failure of regulation to achieve its intended results. The failure has been shown by one curious feature of Labor Department statistics: days lost per worker in American industry due to serious job accidents and health hazards have consistently risen in recent years, whereas the federal government's regulatory activities in the workplace have been expanding. In 1975 the number of workdays lost to injuries and illness rose to 56.2 per 100 workers from 53.1 in 1974. In 1976 the rise continued: about 60.5 days per 100 workers were lost.[11] It turns out that the number of job-related injuries has been declining during the period. How does that square with the rise in time lost? The answer would seem to reflect little credit on OSHA: the agency has succeeded in reducing the trivial accidents which account for little lost time. Meanwhile, the toll from the more serious accidents continues to mount.

A more satisfying way to produce a safer work environment would be to bring about a change in *approach* to regulation. If the objective of public policy is to reduce accidents, the policy should focus directly on reduction of accidents. Excessively detailed regulations often are merely a substitute for hard policy decisions. Rather than issue citations to employers who fail to fill out the forms correctly or who do not post the correct notices, the emphasis would be placed on employers who actually have the worst safety records. In short, the change in approach to regulation would involve a more concerted effort to identify priorities—serious problems, not ancillary items—and then correcting the problems.

But the government should not be concerned with how a specific company achieves the objective of a safer working environment. After all, more accidents are caused by human error than by inadequate safety devices. Carelessness, fatigue, boredom, and anger take their toll. Some companies may thus find it more efficient to change work rules; others may find that the best route is to retrain workers. Making operational business decisions is precisely what government should avoid, but that is what now dominates so many regulatory programs. Moreover, without diminishing the responsibility of the employers, the sanctions under the federal occupational safety and health law should be extended to employees, especially those whose negligence endangers other employees. The purpose here is not to be harsh to individuals, but to set up fair and effective incentives.

ALTERNATIVES TO REGULATION

Government has available various powers other than regulation. Through its taxing authority, it can provide strong signals to the market and hence to both businesses and consumers. In the environmental area, much of the current dependence on direct controls could be shifted to utilizing the more indirect but powerful incentives available through the price system via use of the tax device. Pollution taxes would be such a mechanism; they would increase the prices of highly polluting means of production and consumption and thus encourage shifts to more ecologically sound production and consumption patterns. Imaginative use of such excise taxation could encourage some modification of existing and planned industrial, commercial, residential, and even government facilities.

The desired results would not be accomplished by fiat, but rather by making the high-pollutant product or service more expensive than the low-pollutant product or service. The basic guiding principle in that area would simply be that people and institutions do not pollute because they get a positive enjoyment from abusing the environment. Rather, they pollute because it is easier, cheaper, or more profitable to do so. In lieu of a corps of inspectors or regulators, we would use the price system to make polluting harder, more expensive, and less profitable.

Fees for discharging effluents into bodies of water would encourage more extensive efforts to improve pollution abatement by those who can do so at relatively low cost (and thus avoid paying the fees); less antipollution effort would be made by those for whom the costs of reducing pollution would be greater than the required fees. Thus, on balance, pollution control taxation could provide an equally effective but less costly mechanism than the existing regulatory standards approach to achieving the desired ecological objectives.

There is a parallel here to the operation of a tariff system. Even a tariff instituted ostensibly only for revenue purposes keeps some products out of the United States to the extent that demand and supply respond at all to price changes. And the higher the tariff on a product, the closer it comes to becoming a protective tariff that keeps the undesired item out entirely.

Other regulatory objectives might benefit from the kind of fundamental rethinking implicit in this line of reasoning. For example, the current emphasis on putting ever more complicated safety equipment in the automobile may be a more costly alternative to achieving a higher degree of motor vehicle safety than tougher enforcement of existing traffic laws. The data show that most fatal accidents involve a driver or a pedestrian who has been drinking. Such action is not effectively dealt with by mandating more equipment on the automobile.[12]

It may be useful indeed to shift the focus of social regulation from almost sole attention to the business firm to include the discretion and responsibility of the consumer. For example, many public interest groups are concerned with "openness" in large organizations, both public and private, and especially with the provision of more information. In the area of public concern with corporate performance, there may be considerable opportunity for greater reliance on an information strategy as an alternative or supplement to detailed regulation. The more widespread provision of information to consumers on potential hazards in various products may, in many circumstances, be far more effective than banning specific products or setting standards requiring expensive alterations in existing products. The information approach takes account of the great variety of consumer needs, as well as the desires of individuals to make up their own minds. When a sample of consumers was asked, in January 1978, whether government should restrict the sale of foods and drugs that it thinks dangerous, 52 percent responded negatively, desiring instead to let people make their own decisions.[13]

More widespread dissemination of comparative accident statistics may set in motion pressures for individual companies to provide a safer working environment than their competitors. Similar data on product-associated accidents might encourage firms to devote more attention to safety in the design of the goods that they sell. The underlying assumption here is that, rather than put sole reliance on government intervention, it may be desirable to let informed consumers make the deliberate choices among products with different safety and other qualitative characteristics. But as in most other areas of government-business relations, a sense of balance is needed: information is not a free good, and more may not always be better than less; the trivial may obscure the important.

A related question has to do with the limits of government responsibility for individual actions. For example, the staff of the Federal Trade Commission argues that the Commission, via restrictive regulation, should protect children from any harmful effects of television advertising because many parents are reluctant to take the "drastic" step of turning off the television set.[14] Should that proposal be adopted by the Commission, the federal government literally would wind up with the role of Big Mother!

Surely, as we have found out, it just is not practicable for government to attempt to regulate every facet of private behavior. That need not constitute a plea for anarchy. Indeed, as stated before, it is important that government do well the various important tasks that it undertakes, from which it follows that Congress and state and local legislatures must choose carefully the tasks that they assign to government. The pertinent question is not whether there are shortcomings in the private sector. Of course, the human beings involved in the operation of the American business system are fallible and the results of their activities do not always conform to the prevailing notions of what is in the public welfare. The serious question is whether, in view of the many goals of our society, government regulation in a particular instance will do more good than harm.

A cleaner environment, for example, is a very important national objective, but surely many sensible and inherently necessary trade-offs must be made (that is, cleaner air versus cleaner water, ecological improvements versus energy conservation, and so forth). Thus, the all-or-nothing approach—zero discharge of pollutants—should not be viewed as a feasible objective or even a sensible goal. The same sense of balance would help in each of the other regulatory programs.

References

1. "Record Lows in Public Confidence," *Current Opinion,* January 1976.
2. "Ratings of Ethical Standards for Several Occupations," *Current Opinion,* September 1976.
3. *Gallup Opinion Index,* March 1977, Report No. 140, pp. 10,11,16.
4. "Key Congressional Economist Doesn't See '79 Recession, or Improved Inflation Rate," *The Wall Street Journal,* July 12, 1978.
5. Comptroller General of the United States, *New Interstate Truckers Should Be Granted Temporary Operating Authority More Readily* (Washington, D.C.: General Accounting Office, CED-78-32, February 24, 1978), pp. 6–15.
6. "Diamond Meat-Tray Manufacturer Closing Upstate Plant in Wake of New York City Law on Packaging," *The New York Times,* May 28, 1978.
7. Michael Sterne, "Environmentalist Questions Priorities," *The New York Times,* May 12, 1978.
8. William Robbins, "Experts Cite a Way to End Grain Blasts," *The New York Times,* July 13, 1978.
9. See James C. Miller III, "Lessons of the Economic Impact Statement Program," *Regulation,* July–August 1977.
10. An example is S. 600, the proposed Regulatory Reform Act of 1977 (the Percy-Byrd-Ribicoff bill).
11. "Job-Related Injuries, Illnesses and Deaths Fell Substantially in 1975, Agency Says," *The Wall Street Journal,* December 9, 1976; Labor Agency to Revoke Job-Safety Rules It Believes Are Burdensome, Ineffective," *The Wall Street Journal,* December 2, 1977.
12. Murray L. Weidenbaum, *Business, Government, and the Public* (Englewood Cliffs, N.J.: Prentice-Hall, 1977), p. 51.
13. "Opinion Roundup," *Public Opinion,* May–June 1978.
14. "The FTC and Children's Advertising," *Regulation,* May–June 1978.

5

The Shape of Things to Come: A Pessimistic Perspective

The issue is broader than "government regulation of business." It's government regulation of consumers . . . of employees . . . of state and local governments . . . of stockholders, government regulation of everybody.
James C. Miller III
American Enterprise Institute

IT may be easy, far too easy, to develop enthusiasm for proposals which would streamline regulatory programs or economize on the use of government power. So many of the pressures for change, however, would demand and produce opposite results. The second fundamental approach to change in business-government relations involves government far more deeply in the day-to-day functioning of the American business system. Examples of proposals of that nature are numerous and have been given varying degrees of public support. They range from altering the basic organizational structure of the modern corporation to adopting a centralized planning mechanism. An examination of the major proposals along those lines provides useful insight into the setting in which American business would operate if some of those proposals were enacted into law.

INCREASING THE GOVERNMENT'S CHARTERING POWER

Many so-called corporate activists would use government power to charter corporations to alter the basic function and organization of the modern corporation. Specific suggestions range from restructuring corporate boards of directors to include large numbers of representatives of designated interest groups to mandating public reporting of various business functions deemed to involve "social responsibility."

Ralph Nader has developed a set of the most ambitious and far-reaching proposals to restructure the American corporation.[1] To achieve what he terms the "popularization" of the corporation, he would rewrite the rules governing corporation chartering. He advocates the assumption by the federal government of the chartering power now given the individual states.

Under the Nader proposals, the federal government would then broaden the current disclosure requirements of the Securities and Exchange Commission to cover "the whole impact of the corporation on society." Nader would also require each company to establish a procedure for handling complaints. The complaints would be categorized and fed into a national computerized system from which they would be instantaneously available to all citizens. Although he acknowledges that "this sounds like Buck Rogers," Nader urges the establishment of a mass information system that would cover such other areas as the research each company is doing and the topics of that research. He also would open corporate tax returns to public inspection because, in Nader's words, "a corporation does not have the right of privacy, like an individual."

For corporations beyond a "certain" size or having a "dominant" position in a market, Nader would require that approximately one-fourth of the board of directors be chosen in national elections. Individual directors would be assigned responsibility for specific areas of concern, such as the environment or employee relations. In his concept, federal chartering would develop a "constitutionalism" for corporate employees, and provide various protections for "whistle blowers" who object to specific company activities. He has also urged a mandatory mail plebiscite of shareholders on all "fundamental" transactions.

The sum of his reforms, Nader acknowledges, is a concept of "social bankruptcy" whereby a company would be thrown into receivership if it failed to meet its "social" obligations. What Nader does not acknowledge—at least not overtly—is the massive scale of public involvement and private expense that would flow from his far-reaching reforms. All that is apart from the technical impracticality of carrying out his visionary schemes.

Moreover, to suggest the assignment to each board member of responsibility for one sphere of a company's activities is to demonstrate a fundamental misunderstanding of the operations of any large organization. The suggestion runs counter to the management principle of delegating authority to operating officials who, in turn, are responsible to and accountable for their performance to a superior review body. That overseer function is, of course, a basic activity of the corporation's board of directors.

More modest proposals for change in the structure of the American corporation have come from other sources. Harold Williams, chairman of the Securities and Exchange Commission and former dean of the Graduate School of Management at UCLA, contends that the ideal board of directors would include only one company officer, the chief executive. All other board members, including the chairman, would be chosen from outside the company. Williams's concept of outside directors excludes bankers, lawyers, or anyone else having business dealings with the company. In his view, outside-dominated boards could do a better job of representing the stockholders' long-term interests than executives who are responsible for day-to-day management.

Williams, unlike Nader, would not allocate individual directorships to representatives of employees, consumers, minorities, or other groups. "It would be disastrous. . . . Constituency representation . . . makes the board a political body," according to Williams.[2] When asked whether his proposal infringes on private property rights, the SEC chairman stated that corporations are more than economic institutions owned by shareholders. "Corporate America is too important, and perceived as too powerful, to fail to address the kinds of issues that are noneconomic."

A third set of proposals was set forth by a distinguished group of business, academic, and professional leaders convened by the American Assembly in April 1978. The group urged that corporations take the initiative in responding to the changing environment facing business and thus minimize the need for government action. Contending that companies often lag in recognizing the significance of new voices, the Assembly's report stated that managers must be made more aware of their various publics, more sensitive to shifting expectations, and more alert to new claimants for corporate attention and service.

The Assembly focused on the corporate board as having a primary role in interpreting society's expectations and standards for management. The majority of board members, it urged, should come from outside the company management and be unencumbered by relationships which limit their independence. The report specifically recommended that key inside managers, in addition to the chief executive, remain eligible to serve; it pointed out several important strengths that they possess. The strengths include bringing the board's perspectives into the discharge of regular duties and helping outside members evaluate possible successors to the chief executive. The Assembly did recommend that a corporation's chief executive officer not serve as chairman of the board. The American Assembly also pointed out that effective self-regulation requires oversight mechanisms to set standards, monitor compliance, and insure that self-regulation does not become self-serving in restraint of trade.[3]

The three proposals for restructuring American corporations share a strong notion of public accountability. Each takes the fundamental approach of changing both the composition and function of corporate directorships; each to a varying degree would make some aspect of "private" management more "public." In the case of Nader's proposals, corporations would become quasi-nationalized public holdings run by elected officials. The procedure would alter a large section of what we have come to know as free enterprise. The proposals of Williams and the American Assembly work in the same direction but in a more moderate way and with an eye toward the corporations' own capabilities for self-regulation.

Although it may be unlikely that any current set of proposals for the reform of corporate governance will be adopted in its present form—whether Nader's or Williams's or the American Assembly's—it would not be at all surprising if some significant portion of the proposals were put into effect either by force in the form of government regulation or voluntarily to avoid such overt action by government.

Two recent actions by the Securities and Exchange Commission serve as illustrations of the forcible approach to reform. In May 1978 it was reported that the SEC was investigating the adequacy of U.S. Steel's disclosures relating to environmental matters. That seems to be a step in the direction of Ralph Nader's proposal for disclosing "the whole impact" of the corporation on society. And, more importantly, in June 1978 the SEC announced that it had taken the first steps toward requiring American companies to disclose a wide variety of information about what their directors do for them. The rules being drafted by the Commission include disclosure of the following wide array of data:

- The composition and function of committees of directors that nominate other directors and executives, set pay, or oversee financial records.
- The existence of personal or business relations between directors and management. Directors would have to be classified as management directors, affiliated management directors (such as the company's outside lawyer), and unaffiliated nonmanagement directors (that is, people who have nothing to do with the company).
- The reason a director resigns, if due to a policy dispute.

- Information about attendance at board meetings, possibly identifying directors who do not attend a certain percentage of meetings.
- The total number of directorships held by directors, as well as identification of directorships that may pose a conflict of interest.
- Fees to directors.

The SEC stated that some of the disclosures would have to be in proxy statements sent to shareholders and other information may have to be reported to the Commission itself, as in a firm's annual report. The SEC commissioners prefer that companies take on the "reform" task themselves by appointing more independent directors to their boards and by establishing independent audit committees. Also, the Commission believes that if companies are required to disclose the existence of audit committees, that will induce other firms which do not have such committees to establish them.[4]

Some important changes in the structure of the corporation are already under way. For example, a significant shift is occurring in the composition of the boards of directors of American companies, especially the larger ones. In the case of the 500 largest industrial corporations (the *Fortune* 500), the number of outside directors rose from 3,049 in 1967 to 3,436 in 1977, although the total number of directors declined. The number of current executives on those corporate boards dropped from 2,868 to 2,332 during the decade, as did retired managers, from 277 to 227.[5]

It is important to realize, as economist Ursula Guerrieri has pointed out, that companies operating under any of the proposed federal chartering requirements would tend to have higher costs. If, for example, a corporation were not permitted to relocate its plants in lower-cost areas because either employees or the community vetoed the action, the company would be prevented from improving its competitive position. Management's ability to pursue cost-reducing actions would be constrained in many ways. Capital would continue to flow to corporations which offered the highest earnings, but those earnings might represent only the corporation's superior ability to respond to government regulations. The resulting misallocation of resources would be borne by society as a whole in the form of lowered production of goods and services and thus lowered living standards.[6]

Restructuring the corporation via the government's chartering power, however, is not the only important change in government involvement in business decision making that may be in the offing.

SPLITTING UP THE LARGER COMPANIES

In 1975, then Senators Philip Hart and Hugh Scott introduced in Congress the Antitrust Improvements Act, which would have required the breaking up of large corporations in markets where four or fewer firms hold dominating positions. Although that main part of the Hart-Scott bill did not pass, another provision was enacted into law. That was the section of the bill that allows the attorney general of any state to file antitrust suits against companies to collect triple damages on behalf of the citizens of that state.

Similar proposed action in the antitrust field was that of the Senate Judiciary Committee, which, in June 1976, tentatively approved the so-called Petroleum Industry Competition Act. The Act would require the breakup of 18 of the nation's largest oil companies into separate production, refining, transportation, and marketing entities. The bill subsequently died in committee. During the same year, the Senate Commerce Committee held hearings on a more general proposal to split up large business firms. In late 1977, the Senate Judiciary Committee requested views on the desirability of forcing the major oil companies to rid themselves of their coal and uranium subsidiaries.

In addition, the House Communications Subcommittee proposed in June 1978 a floor-to-ceiling overhaul of the Federal Communications Act. It would require the American Telephone and Telegraph Company to divest itself of its manufacturing subsidiary, Western Electric, and it would likewise force a split-up of General Telephone and Electronics Corporation's telephone and manufacturing operations.

According to AT&T's William M. Ellinghaus, the proposed divestiture would "slow technological innovation, increase the cost of facilities, and lead eventually to higher rates for service." [7] Significantly, it is a debatable point among economists whether the divestiture of Western Electric would hinder or help independent manufacturers of telephone equipment. Since Western Electric (with over $8 billion in sales in 1977) is many times the size of other firms, it would be an imposing competitor if it were turned loose on the market. Economies of scale might enable the company to offer equipment at lower prices than other firms, although that might not necessarily be true of every product line that it offers. In any event, a newly spun-off Western Electric would probably continue to be the major supplier of telephone equipment in America. Conceivably, it could wind up with a larger market share than it now holds.

Clearly, the divestiture issue is not about to disappear. And although breaking up "mammoth" corporations might be expected to have some inherent appeal in an intellectual atmosphere in which small is considered beautiful, there is limited logical support for the position. There are no data, for example, to show that smaller firms are any less likely to engage in misleading advertising or maintain hazardous working conditions or produce unsafe products than larger firms. On the contrary, large corporations frequently have been innovators in establishing high standards of product quality, job safety, environmental protection, and other social concerns. Since virtually every one of those areas is already the subject of detailed federal regulation, it is ironic that the failure of government regulation to achieve its many aims is used to justify the extension of government power over yet other areas of business decision making.

One other important fact weakens the case for the divestiture approach to antitrust: There is no evidence in the economic literature, as Guerrieri points out, that firm size is correlated with monopoly power.[8] A corporation may be large only in absolute terms because of economies of scale, patent rights, or the sheer size of the market in which it operates. Richard M. Cyert, former dean of the business school and now president of Carnegie-Mellon University, testified before a congressional committee dealing with those questions that "Frequently, the reforms suggested have no relationship to the problem. It is like recommending open heart surgery for the cure of the common cold." [9]

Here is a major case in point. Although public concern with oil industry prices and profits has slackened, there is still support for legislation requiring oil firms to divest themselves of large portions of their current activities and limit their investment in new energy areas. That is an instance of "the closer you get, the worse it looks," since proposed action of that sort would be counterproductive. For example, from time to time proposals are made to require the major petroleum companies to spin off their interests in other forms of energy such as coal and uranium. The legislation would make more difficult the task of the private sector to finance the desired expansion of the domestic supply of energy, although that would not be the intent of the law. Forced divestiture would result in a protracted divestment process during the course of which great uncertainty would be generated. Negative effects would be felt by labor, management, shareholders, and customers.

Managements would likely hold "caretaker" positions during that period of uncertainty. New undertakings would generally be postponed. There is a precedent: the prolonged negotiations involved in the forced divestiture of Peabody Coal Company by Kennecott Copper during the middle 1970s. Should the constitutionality of the divestiture legislation be challenged in the courts—a highly likely event—a protracted period of litigation would follow. If several companies were to be simultaneously involved in forced liquidation of their coal and uranium interests, it is hard not to conjure up a condition of turmoil in those two important sectors of energy production. The result likely would be just the reverse of that intended by the proponents of divestiture: a much higher level of oil imports.

It could also be expected that industries other than energy would be afraid that Congress would order the splitting up of their major companies. After all, energy production has a far less concentrated market structure than many other large industries in the United States. In 1976, for example, the output of the eight largest mining corporations accounted for only 34 percent of the United States production of bituminous and lignite coal. Coal firms owned by oil companies accounted for only 17 percent of coal production. In contrast, the top four industrial firms produce 90 percent or more of locomotives, cereals, aircraft, photocopiers, toothpaste, soaps and detergents, cameras, film, soup, and chocolate candy.

But issues other than economic ones are involved here. Corporations are created and sustained by freedom of association and contract. The source of those freedoms is individual rights. Therefore, it is important to remember, as Robert Hessen states, that "Rights are not suddenly forfeited when a business grows beyond some arbitrarily defined size." [10] That, by the way, is a basic point that consumer activists have at times tossed to the winds. The compulsory restructuring of the American corporation would represent an unintentional but important dilution of private property rights. And that dilution would not occur via the formal loss of the forms of ownership rights; it would occur because of the increased difficulty in effectively *exercising* those rights. Since the freedom and ability to use one's rights is what constitutes "liberty," it may be helpful—if not necessary—to keep in mind a remark made by the economist and noted author Henry Hazlitt: "Too many of us make a mistake in treating 'liberty' merely in the singular, or merely as an abstraction. Our liberty is made up, in action, of a thousand specific liberties. Men seldom lose their liberty all at once." [11]

EXPANDING GOVERNMENT OPERATIONS AFFECTING BUSINESS

Numerous proposals have been and are being made for new federal undertakings that are not, in themselves, intended to alter the basic relations between government and business but would nevertheless have the effect of producing great changes. Obvious examples are the plans to establish a comprehensive national health insurance system operated by the federal government. Those plans focus on the expanded delivery of health care to the entire American population and inevitably attempt to deal with the sharp escalation in medical costs that has been occurring. The proposals are generally intended to rectify the cost problem by enforcing detailed control mechanisms not only over health care professionals but also over the industries which supply health care products and services.[12]

In this instance, the indirect but powerful effect on business of expanded government programs can be seen in the frequently encountered subject of control of prices charged for medicines, especially prescription drugs. Although the intent of any national health insurance plan would not be to regulate the prices which privately owned pharmaceutical houses charge for their products, the thrust of many of the programs' proposed rules is squarely in that direction. Similar effects would be felt by such other industries producing health care products as manufacturers of scientific instruments and medical equipment. Thus the nationwide effects of a proposed law ostensibly dealing with personal health care could actually constitute another expansion of government power over the ability of the American business system to manufacture and distribute the products that it develops.

In a closely related but more direct way, the proposed Drug Regulation Reform Act of 1978 outlines a new and conceivably pernicious role for government in private scientific activities. The bill's key feature would be the wide discretionary powers which the Food and Drug Administration could henceforth use both in deciding whether to approve a new drug and in forcing drug manufacturers to use broad and ambiguous standards in planning and conducting their research. The bill would permit the FDA to decide which new drug research would be promoted and which discouraged, to define how scientific experiments should be planned and executed, and to exercise other controls over the clinical research performed by private companies. In essence, the bill has the purpose of moving the federal government from a role of evaluator and judge of private industry's research to one of controller and director of it.[13]

But a national health insurance plan and the Drug Reform Bill are only two of the government proposals that would, if adopted, have indirect but adverse effects on the private sector. There have been, for example, several controversial proposals in Congress for a new federal Agency for Consumer Advocacy (ACA). The bills would create an independent agency in the executive branch ostensibly designed to intervene in federal regulatory and legal proceedings on behalf of the "consumer" or the "public interest." [14]

Such an agency would duplicate the activities of literally hundreds of units of the government which look after consumer-related concerns. But its effects on business, and subsequently on the economy and the standard of living, could be to reduce the private sector's incentive to create new sources of supply and thereby prolong shortages of products and ultimately raise prices. Such a regulatory agency as the ACA, by being responsive to the *short-run* demands of consumer groups who are oblivious to the economic impact of their positions, would operate to the detriment not only of the public interest but also of the long-run consumer interest as well. Senator John Tower of Texas has made clear those adverse impacts—on business and on the consumer who is supposedly being "advocated"—in the following way:

> Most agencies will . . . when they are faced with the [ACA] . . . cave in to the shortrun consumer goal of trying to keep goods and services at minimum prices and maximum quality, rather than at prices and qualities that market forces determine will give the consumer the most for his money. Governmental decisions based on shortrun consumer interests will in most instances paradoxically result ultimately in a reduction in supplies and quality of the goods and services in question. New and improved supplies will be called forth then only after a substantial increase in capital outlay is made to offset the economic disruption involved in the corruption of the market system, with the short-sighted, solely consumer-oriented governmental action.[15]

Still other proposals for expanded government operations point to unfavorable and indirect repercussions on U.S. business. One of them is the so-called Labor Law Reform Act, introduced in the Senate in 1978, by which the National Labor Relations Act would be amended to give labor unions significant new powers in organizing their campaigns, elections, and collective bargaining procedures on first contracts. The bill would mandate "equal access" for unions—that is, employers would be forced to allow unions to solicit members on company time and property whenever an employer discusses unionization. Stiff penalties are stipulated in the bill only for business violations, not for union violations of labor laws. The Small Business Administration, moreover, has reported that small businesses would be disproportionately hard hit by the proposal, since 75 percent of all representation elections involve units of 50 or fewer employees.[16]

But perhaps the most extensive expansion of government power over the economy is occurring via the poorly understood phenomenon of government credit programs. The programs are usually viewed as painless, if not costless, ways for government to provide financial support for some part of society. But the result is that the use of a rising share of private saving is being determined by government. Proposed new federal credit programs range from guaranteeing the bonds of hard-pressed central city governments to subsidizing the financing of new domestic energy sources. Under any of the proposals, the federal government would be directing more and more of the flow of investment capital in the United States. That inherently is a function which is basic to the future of a capitalistic economy.

If we have learned anything from this country's experience with government operation of credit programs, it is that the programs are not "free." Numerous costs to taxpayers and consumers result when the federal government guarantees securities issued by other institutions, public or private. The federal credit programs increase the total amount of federally designated borrowings (which includes the public debt), and thus they cause an increase in the interest rates which are paid on those borrowings to attract the funds from the private sector. That results in an increase in the interest rates which the Treasury pays on the public debt.

In the process, other borrowers get squeezed out of the credit market. After all, government credit programs do not increase the total amount of saving that occurs in the United States; they merely give one borrower a preferred position over another. From past experience it is clear who suffers in the process: new and small businesses, prospective homeowners, and local governments that do not have the federal help.[17]

ADOPTING A COMPREHENSIVE "INCOMES" POLICY

Dissatisfaction with continuing high levels of inflation and unemployment has led to a rising chorus of advocacy of what are called incomes policies. This type of government intervention in business decision making has been used widely in Western Europe and on occasion in this country. Unlike the traditional tools of monetary and fiscal policy which tend to affect the economy indirectly, incomes policy means that the government is participating directly in the private business decisions which eventually determine how much income an individual receives from his or her total economic activities.

Incomes policies cover a broad spectrum of alternatives ranging from presidential "jawboning" against individual wage and price increases, to voluntary adherence to federal guidelines on wages and prices, to actual government control over specific wage and price changes. As a result, the free market may be viewed as one end of a spectrum of incomes policies and comprehensive and compulsory wage and price controls as the other end.

In the period 1971–1973, the federal government moved initially to a position of almost complete control over wages and prices; subsequently, it returned gradually to the more conventional situation of reliance on competitive markets. Even though that situation may not be repeated, we may see instead a series of steps that constitute a gradual and reluctant "backing into" government intervention.

Such a state of affairs would not be anything new, nor would it be desirable. In the words of Professor Robert Lanzillotti of the University of Florida, who served as a governmental price controller in 1971–1973, although the historical record on incomes policy is quite old, "age has not helped the success rate." [18] In Babylonian history there are vague references to wage and price controls instituted some 4,000 years ago. The most extensive early attempt at such measures was Diocletian's *Edict on Prices* in A.D. 301. It contained a preamble littered with phrases attacking Roman businessmen that are reminiscent of the way many current politicians refer to business: "merchants of immense fortune . . . greedy and full of lust for plunder . . . uncurbed passion for gain."

Apparently, Diocletian's edict had little impact on inflation in his day, and eventually it was rescinded. Similar experiments in incomes policy have been recorded by historians in more recent periods; each has ended with similar results. In Lanzillotti's words, the experience of most Western industrialized countries which have utilized wage and price controls has been to discard them because of "unbearable" economic contradictions.

Current interest in incomes policies in the United States centers on two different uses of the tax system by Congress to "encourage" business and labor to conform to what would be government-issued guidelines for acceptable wage and price increases. The first procedure, the "stick" approach, would impose a tax penalty on firms that grant wage increases in excess of the government's guidelines. It is supposed to provide employers with an "incentive" to resist excessive wage demands. The "carrot" approach would provide tax relief to both employees and business firms who keep their wage and price increases within the stipulated guidelines. Both tax-based incomes policies have been subjected to much criticism. The most devastating, although perhaps unintentional, criticism was leveled by the staff of the U.S. Treasury Department which examined the practical feasibility of such controls.

The staff pointed out that if a stick-approach tax penalty is imposed for only one year, it is likely to have very arbitrary effects on firms depending on when the firm customarily raises wages and prices. One Treasury official remarked that "complicated intra-year adjustments annualizing wage and price increases" would be needed to reduce the arbitrariness of the program. He then went on to point out that if the program were temporary, firms and workers might simply avoid the penalties by agreeing to postpone the high wage increases until after the program expired. Unwittingly, therefore, the staff highlighted a basic and ludicrous pitfall of any "temporary" incomes policies when it concluded the best way to avoid that problem is to state at the outset that the tax-based incomes policy will be extended.[19] In essence, then, any "temporary" control of wages and prices would have to become permanent if it were to be effective.

In the case of the carrot approach, the Treasury staff found other difficulties. As it stated euphemistically, "providing tax reductions for workers raises some vexing administrative problems." Companies would have to inform their employees on the W-2 tax-withholding form that they qualify for the tax break that is the result of following wage and price guidelines. If, on audit, it were found that the workers did not qualify, the Internal Revenue Service would have to collect from the firm. In the Treasury's words, "This solution is practical, but it seems to suggest that employees are responsible for successful wage restraint, while companies are to blame for any failure." So much for the equity of incomes policies between business and labor.

Quite clearly, should the federal government launch an incomes policy in earnest, it would represent yet another expansion and complication of government involvement in internal business decision making. The intervention would be futile, inequitable, or both. Yet that does not exhaust the possibilities for further federal intervention into the detailed workings of the private economy. The advent of a national planning system would represent the most ambitious expansion of the economic role of government.

ESTABLISHING A CENTRALIZED PLANNING SYSTEM

Advocates of proposals to establish a national economic planning system for the United States contend that, if it is acceptable for business, planning ought to be equally acceptable for government. That is such a simple proposition that it seems self-evident—or at least almost so. Yet fundamental differences exist between public and private planning. Comparison of the two provides an idea of what "planning" is all about, for we are dealing with the difference between (1) forecasting and reacting to the future and (2) trying to regulate the future. Corporate planning of necessity is based on attempting to persuade the rest of society to purchase the goods and services produced by a given firm; the controls that may accompany the plan are internally oriented. In striking contrast, since government is sovereign, its planning ultimately involves coercion, that is, the use of its power to achieve the results that it desires. Its controls are thus externally oriented; they extend their sway over the entire society.

The essence of the difference between public and private planning is the locus of decision making. If Ford or General Motors or Chrysler is not selling as many automobiles as it had planned, there is a limited number of things it can do. It can, within its available resources, lower the price or change the nature of the product. But, as evidenced by the demise of the Edsel, the LaSalle, and the DeSoto, it may at times simply be forced to abandon the project. The consumer remains the ultimate decision maker.

The situation is far different in the public sector. Compared with the largest private corporation, there are more options available to the government. If the government does not think that the American public is buying enough cars, it can lower the price to the consumer as much as it likes via tax reductions—down to zero if it so determines. Alternatively, it can purchase outright the output of the automobile industry or simply take over the ownership of the industry.

The Humphrey-Javits bill and the original Humphrey-Hawkins bill were two attempts to institute a centralized U.S. planning system embracing the economic activities of both the public and the private sectors. Although neither bill got beyond the stage of congressional hearings, interest in planning legislation continues.

The Humphrey-Hawkins bill itself, however, has been revised to downplay the planning mechanism and emphasize setting goals for full employment and for other social objectives ranging from environmental improvement to enhancing Indian welfare.

Simultaneously, attention is being given in some intellectual circles to other ways to fundamentally expand government direction of the economy. An example is the work of the Exploratory Project for Economic Alternatives. That private group has developed highly publicized plans for a "sweeping reorganization" of the major corporate and government institutions in the economy "to produce economic security and economic democracy." [20] The Project's plans would, on the basis of the most preliminary reading, fundamentally alter the balance of functions and power between the public and private sectors in the United States.

The advocates of national economic planning who base their case on an extension of business planning activities overestimate the state of the art in the private sector. It is apparent that no amount of formalized planning has eliminated any company's uncertainty concerning future technological change, the vagaries of weather, discoveries of energy or other natural resources, outbreaks of war, assassinations of national leaders, or even shifts in the desires of the sometimes fickle consumer.

But even discounting the shortcomings of existing business planning techniques, the differences between business and government decision making are fundamental. Despite all the sophisticated apparatus, business planning is based on the traditional assumption that the ultimate decisions on the allocation of resources in the society are to be made by individual consumers. An important corollary is that a company, if it guesses wrong on what consumers will buy, will suffer the consequences.

In sharp contrast, government planning, implicitly or explicitly, is based on a fundamentally different set of assumptions. Government determines what it considers to be in the society's overall interests. If the public does not respond accordingly, it is not the planners who are considered to be at fault. Rather, new and more effective devices must be developed to make the public accommodate the planners' view of the good (or great) society.

In essence, then, in government planning the consumers (or the public at large) do *not* make the ultimate decisions in planning, though they *are* forced to suffer the consequences.

In its simplest terms, business planning is part of a decentralized decision-making process in which the individual makes the ultimate choices. National planning is a centralized process in which the key economic decisions are made in the form of government rulings. The greatest danger of centralized economic planning is that, if adopted, it will—perhaps unintentionally at first, but inevitably as its initial results prove disappointing— propel the society away from market freedoms and toward greater government controls over individual behavior.[21]

CONCLUSION

Surely there is a strong likelihood that government will exercise a growing influence over business decision making in the United States, yet that trend is not inevitable. The outcome will depend both on business reactions to the underlying situation and on the changing views of the many other interest groups involved. Those possibilities for change are the subject of the rest of this book.

The prospects for private enterprise in the United States a decade from now might conceivably be more favorable than they are today. Economic developments rarely follow a straight line for any length of time. So, at some point in the next ten years, a major reaction to the rising tide of government intervention may occur. It may become increasingly apparent to the public that the aggregate effect of the myriad of government actions is negative rather than positive—that the cure often is worse than the disease.

Surely, government will continue to exercise a large influence over business decision making. Yet it is *not* inevitable that the current tendency toward increased involvement in detailed, internal business actions will proceed without modification. With the raising of formal and informal levels of business accountability, there may be a lessened desire on the part of the various interest groups and legislators to specify closely the exact procedures that business must follow to attain important national objectives. That changed attitude will require a good deal of restraint as well as a new outlook on the part of business, public interest groups, and government officials.

References

1. Eileen Shanahan, "Business Change: Nader Interview," *The New York Times,* January 24, 1971.
2. Harold M. Williams, *Corporate Accountability,* An Address to the Fifth Annual Securities Regulation Institute, San Diego, Calif.: January 18, 1978; Leonard Wiener, "A New Look for Corporate Boards," *St. Louis Globe Democrat,* March 2, 1978.
3. American Assembly, *Corporate Governance in America* (New York: Columbia University, 1978).
4. "SEC Acts to Require Disclosures by Firm Directors, but Delays Other Decisions," *The Wall Street Journal,* June 8, 1978.
5. Lee Smith, "The Boardroom Is Becoming a Different Scene," *Fortune,* May 8, 1978.
6. Ursula A. Guerrieri, "Economic Issues Raised by the Federal Corporate Chartering Proposal," *Business Economics,* May 1978.
7. "Communications Law Overhaul Is Being Proposed," *The Wall Street Journal,* June 8, 1978.
8. Guerrieri, op. cit., p. 70.
9. "Statement of Richard M. Cyert," in U.S. Senate, Committee on Commerce, *Corporate Rights and Responsibilities,* hearings in June 1976 (Washington, D.C.: GPO, 1976), p. 139.
10. "Statement of Robert Hessen," ibid., p. 11.
11. Henry Hazlitt, quoted in "Onward," *Notes from FEE* (New York: The Foundation for Economic Education, May 1978).
12. See *Health Insurance: What Should Be the Federal Role?* a roundtable held January 22, 1975 (Washington, D.C.: American Enterprise Institute).
13. Gerald D. Laubach, "The Drug Regulation Reform Bill: Will It Facilitate Research?" *National Journal,* May 20, 1978.
14. See *Consumer Protection Legislation* (Washington, D.C.: American Enterprise Institute, April 26, 1977).

15. Ibid., p. 14; quoted from *Congressional Quarterly*, Vol. 31 (Weekly Report, March 31, 1973), p. 723.

16. See *Labor Law Reform?* a roundtable held March 21, 1978 (Washington, D.C.: American Enterprise Institute).

17. For details, see Murray L. Weidenbaum, *An Economic Analysis of the Federal Government's Credit Programs*, Working Paper No. 18 (St. Louis: Washington University Center for the Study of American Business, 1977).

18. Robert F. Lanzillotti, *Price and Wage Controls: The U.S. Experience* (Gainesville, Fla.: University of Florida, College of Business Administration, 1977), p. 2.

19. *Statement of Emil M. Sunley, Deputy Assistant Secretary of the Treasury for Tax Policy Before the Senate Committee on Banking, Housing, and Urban Affairs* (Washington, D.C.: Department of the Treasury, May 22, 1978), p. 3.

20. Gar Alperovitz and Jeff Faux, "An Economic Program for the Coming Decade," *Democratic Review*, November 1975.

21. See Murray L. Weidenbaum and Linda Rockwood, "Corporate Planning Versus Government Planning," *Public Interest*, Winter 1977.

6

The Business Response: The "Business of Ideas"

The only way that any President can gain the confidence of that [business] community is by turning the country over to it lock, stock, and cash register.
The New Yorker

IF there is any uncertainty about the hostility of the environment in which the typical business firm operates in the United States, the passage quoted above should dispel it. And the quotation is not taken out of context, nor is it from an obscure, radical publication. It is the theme of the lead editorial in one of the nation's most prestigious mass circulation magazines, *The New Yorker*. Although the article appeared in late 1976, similar articles have appeared in many other publications since.

In fact, any issue of a daily newspaper is likely to contain allegations of companies using "misleading" advertising to sell "unsafe" products, "imperialistic" multinational corporations operating uncontrolled "slush" funds, companies "polluting" the environment, forcing their employees to work under "cancer-inducing" conditions, "constantly" raising their prices—and earning "obscene" profits to boot. The charges seem to justify the rapid expansion of government intervention in business that has been cataloged in the preceding chapters. What can or should the business community do about the situation? In practice, three different approaches can be identified.

The first is the simplest. Ralph Nader and his fellow consumer activists say that business should be forced to confess its sins and mend its ways. The second approach is advocated by various trade associations as well as individual business executives: launch a campaign to sell the free enterprise system. That includes hiring advertising firms to sell free enterprise in the same way that they sell corn flakes or underarm deodorants.

Neither of the two approaches is totally wrong. Some of the allegations of the critics are valid. They should be answered with substantive change and not with expanded public relations efforts. Business firms, more often than not, are wasting their time and their shareholders' money by concentrating on polishing their images. Actions do speak louder than words—especially bad actions. A certain amount of positive and factual writing and speechmaking on the benefits of the private enterprise system can be useful, but sole reliance on that approach is insufficient. It invariably places the speechmaker on the defensive and literally forces him to defend every goof on the part of every business executive.

There is a third and more positive response to the attack on the American business system. As a former business planner, voluntarily retired, the author recalls that one of the first steps taken prior to launching a new product is to research the market. To put it bluntly, the market for *ideas* is fundamentally different from the market for the traditional products of business. The differences are pervasive. They include the research and development process, distribution channels, marketing methods, personnel, and the method of financing.

Just think of the major intellectual "products" that led to the tremendous expansion of government controls in the health and safety area. The Muckrakers—Ida Tarbell, Upton Sinclair, and so on—started the trend several generations ago. The 1930s saw the publication of *100 Million Guinea Pigs*. More recently, Rachel Carson wrote *Silent Spring* and Ralph Nader, *Unsafe At Any Speed*.

None of those extremely influential "products" were developed, produced, or marketed through the same channels that business firms are accustomed to use, since, for better or worse, they are products of the intellect. If the pen was mightier than the sword in an earlier day, the typewriter and the printing press are still holding their own today. But let us not concentrate entirely on the mere design and manufacture of the product, or in this case the document.

The channels of distribution are important. None of those items was published by a labor union or an advertising agency or a government bureau or any other obviously self-serving institution. Each apparently was the product of an individual who wrote what he or she believed. Each was widely reviewed and reported in the newspapers and magazines which potential book buyers, and others, read. This is the intellectual arena in which the proponents of the private enterprise system must compete. It is new terrain for many, and successes may be few and far between at the outset. But given the importance of the future of the economic system, business may have no alternative but to make those necessarily innovative and often long-term investments. Many of the actions may at first seem very indirect ways to defend the system, but some patience and investment of resources are surely warranted.

Five major steps or activities can be identified as part of the comprehensive business response.

DOING A BETTER JOB OF MINDING THE STORE

The first and most fundamental response to the widespread public dissatisfaction with the business system is simple, but perhaps not so easily made. It is for American business to do a better job of minding the store. The most basic way to satisfy the American people on a long-term, sustainable basis is for our economic system to produce higher employment, a lower rate of inflation, and a rising standard of living for the average family. There is one key proviso: to do all that in an environment of maximum freedom for the individual. Joseph Nolan, the experienced corporate public affairs officer of Monsanto, states that the essence of improving the business image rests not in trying to conjure up a good story when performance fails, but in "adjusting performance so that there will, in fact, be a good story to tell." [1] Robert Quittmeyer, president of Amstar Corporation, makes a similar point: Business communicates with the public primarily through the products it produces. [2]

Each American business firm needs to use both its capital and the skills of labor more effectively to produce its products at a lower cost and to develop better goods and services for the public. There is no more effective advertising or public relations than a satisfied customer. As pointed out by Elisha Gray II, former chairman of the Whirlpool Corporation and now chairman of the Council of Better Business Bureaus, "We have got to establish the public's confidence in the marketplace before we can establish our credibility." This is clearly a case in which performance is far more important than rhetoric.

This first step does not imply a total lack of concern with social responsibility; it does imply a return of emphasis to the basic economic function of the business system: to meet the needs of the consumer. There surely is a proper role for the "social responsibility" approach. Nevertheless, when the same company sponsors the local ballet and is caught in indefensible bribing positions, that yawning gap between the two actions results in great harm to the individual firm as well as to the business system.

In that regard, Thornton Bradshaw, president of Atlantic Richfield, has reminded us of the obvious, which is too often forgotten in discussions of public policy: corporations are special-purpose economic institutions, which cannot cure all social ills. [3] In many areas, they should not even try. Since the United States is richly endowed with many and varied institutions (public and private, profit-seeking and nonprofit), interest group demands and social change, when desirable, can be accomplished through those many institutions. In some cases, particularly in the social areas, the noneconomic institutions may be more appropriate mechanisms for responding to noneconomic concerns. The fact that business may have some social responsibilities does not, of course, make it a social institution.

An outside observer may be struck by a key aspect of the business system which is usually taken for granted. It is trust. And in the economic sphere one aspect of trust, the functioning of the credit mechanism, is a quiet marvel. People whom we have never seen before and whom we are not likely ever to see again readily extend credit to us because they trust us to repay. It is trust—confidence in the basic honesty of most personal relationships—that is at the heart of our economic system. The worker expects that he or she will be paid for work performed. The company expects to be paid for the commodity or service provided. The consumer expects to receive the quality of product that is purchased.

That is why the flurry of reports about "slush" funds and other instances of corporate wrongdoing is so worrisome. The great majority of business firms were not involved in the illegal activities, but public confidence and trust in the integrity of the business system were damaged nevertheless. Corporate executives may wonder in exasperation why the entire business community is tarred with the illegal and immoral acts of a few. After all, consumers as a class are not branded as untrustworthy merely because there are many shoplifters. Perhaps the answer lies in the response by business to aberrant activities.

It was disconcerting to find the leadership of the American business community so tongue-tied on the occasions of corporate wrongdoing. To make an invidious comparison, if an economist should make an outrageous or inaccurate statement, at least six other economists would publicly criticize the errant fellow, and they would do so without any danger of being denounced for attacking the economics profession. But, sad to say, to criticize in public any action of any business executive is to set yourself up for being condemned as an enemy of free enterprise. To put it bluntly, therefore, the intellectual environment within the business community must be raised. All in all, doing an effective job of minding the store, it turns out, is neither a simple nor an easy task.

REDUCING THE PRIVATE IMPERIAL PRESIDENCY

It is far too easy for business to ask the rest of society to support sensible actions that will strengthen the market economy—less regulation, elimination of union featherbedding practices, reduced hostility on the part of consumer organizations, and so on—so long as the burden of those actions is placed elsewhere than on business. Those of us who advocate the deregulation of natural gas, for example, are motivated to do so because the good that will result in the form of higher production and more effective use of domestic energy supplies will far outweigh the added costs. But, of course, it is the consumer who will bear the added costs in the form of higher prices. Although deregulation makes excellent economic sense, it is easy to see why business, rather than consumer groups, endorses it so enthusiastically.

To be truly creditable, business also needs to advocate actions that are difficult or even distasteful to it. That does not include such counterproductive moves as reducing profits and dividends as a way of "punishing" business for whatever shortcomings it may possess. That would be akin to attempting to cure an illness by starving the patient. What would be useful is a course of action which, although painful to some individual business executives, would not harm but might strengthen the overall business system. That would be analogous to urging a flabby person to undertake a program of corrective exercise.

One specific suggestion which, like tough exercise, would be as unpopular as it would be helpful is to curtail and perhaps dismantle what can be called the imperial presidency in the private sector. After the fashion of several recent occupants of the White House, many members of top management of corporations have acquired so-called perks which smack more of the prerogatives of royalty than of the needs of competitive, profit-maximizing, professional management.

The perks that are often very difficult to justify range from using the company plane for taking the children of executives to college, to entertaining friends at the company's hunting lodge, to requiring employees to wash and wax the personal vehicles of senior management as part of their work for the company. In themselves, none of those items may be large relative to the sales volume or earnings of the companies involved, but they send a powerful message—a negative one—to the public. This criticism is not meant as yet another mindless tirade against business executives nor against the special facilities or activities that are often valid, required, and necessary, such as the use of company planes to fly personnel to remote business locations. To oppose such "perks" would be to oppose the normal functioning of business operations.

Some perks are entirely valid and, in fact, necessary activities found in almost any professional or economic field. What is at stake, in short, in the issue of the private imperial presidency is that excessive and at times ludicrous uses of perks are harmful to businesses themselves. Moreover, the perks are altogether likely to generate sanctions in the form of broad government regulations which restrict not merely the blatantly improper perks but perks in *any* form.

Clearly, then, what is needed within business itself is conscious self-restraint—and, we might add, the sort of professional and ethical integrity in the use of perquisites that should be expected of any responsible official, public or private. Surely, a great many corporations—especially the more visible ones—conduct themselves in a very circumspect and prudent manner. A good example of both self-restraint and accountability on the part of business is the response by the chairman of the board of IBM to a question asked by a stockholder at the company's annual meeting in 1978:

> *What is IBM's policy toward perquisites for officers and directors?*
>
> We do not have any hunting lodges or yachts or vacation homes. We have airplanes and some automobiles that are used for business purposes. In rare instances when those are used for personal business, they are charged for at cost. When one of our executives takes some member of the family along on an IBM airplane for something that is not business-related, the executive is billed at commercial rates.[4]

We should hope that the majority of America's companies conduct themselves in this responsible manner with regard to both the valid and the questionable uses of perquisites.

But, unfortunately, not all companies follow the IBM pattern of behavior. One company was reported to have spent $6,000 for a dinner to entertain the members of its board of directors and various friends and advisers. That company's modest bill of fare, at $200 a plate, included veal, salmon, truffle soup, $150-a-bottle port, and, of course, champagne.[5] The executive of another company used the firm's private jet to fly his pedigreed bull terriers to and from dog shows across the United States and Canada.[6] So the fundamental question here is not whether such expenditures are legal or tax-deductible. Rather, the overriding concern is the harm such actions do in reducing public support for the private business system.

The prospects for the future of private enterprise in the United States surely would be enhanced by raising the prevailing mores, such as those which determine what is a legitimate way of getting and keeping large customers. One example of an exceptionally bad way of doing so has occurred in the trucking and rail freight industries. The Interstate Commerce Commission found that those two industries spend many millions of dollars a year wining and dining shipping agents. In 1975, one rail carrier spent $400,000 on birdseed to feed game on a preserve where shippers were entertained. According to the ICC auditor, "They had those birds trained to do everything but fly down the barrel of your gun." [7] In this case, however, government policy has contributed to the problem. Unable to compete by offering lower prices because of regulatory restrictions, some of the trucking and rail companies compete for customers by offering entertainment (including coverage of gambling losses in Las Vegas) and other inducements to traffic managers.

Business simply must recognize the absolute need for voluntary self-restraint in these matters. There is, of course, a fine line between sensible, legitimate nonmonetary income and the type of perks that readily lend themselves to be cited as management rip-offs of the shareholder or consumer or taxpayer. Business as a whole would be far better off if it leaned heavily to the side of restraint when it comes to using corporate resources to maintain a version of the imperial presidency in the private sector. That, in turn, would create a more receptive public environment for the following steps.

PROVIDING INFORMATION

The third step that needs to be taken to improve the external environment in which American business operates is to give the public a better understanding of the full range of impacts of government involvement in business. That does not mean an uncritical attack on all government regulation. Such an approach is unwarranted and ineffective. The public may not be well informed on business matters, but neither is it so ignorant that it will believe a self-serving statement on the part of business or anyone else if only the message is packaged in a slick and professional manner. That approach has been tried often enough. It does not work.

Nor is this a plea for what is often the conventional response of business executives: to sponsor yet another contest in the high schools or colleges with a $25 savings bond prize to the writer of the best essay on "What the Free Enterprise System Means to Me." That really does not meet the serious problem being discussed here. It simply reinforces the belief of many educators that the typical corporate manager is self-serving as well as unimaginative.

The balanced educational message that is needed is simple; it holds the prospect of substantially improving the environment in which public policy toward business is formulated. It is that (1) government regulation of business has benefits which need to be acknowledged and identified, but that (2) government intervention in the economy also entails great costs and, despite those great costs, often does not achieve its objectives. The public is not aware of regulatory costs, which can be substantial, often avoidable, and of such magnitude that they actually interfere with the achievement of important goals of our society. Moreover, ignoring the costs and other negative side effects of government action results in carrying such action far beyond the point at which benefits to society equal the costs, and that technically is overregulation.

As has been shown in earlier chapters, the costs arising from government regulation are extensive: (1) the cost to the taxpayer for supporting a galaxy of government regulators, (2) the cost to the consumer in the form of higher prices to cover the added expense of producing goods and services under government regulations, (3) the cost to the worker in the form of jobs eliminated by government regulation, (4) the cost to the economy resulting from the loss of smaller enterprises which cannot afford to meet the onerous burdens of government regulation, and (5) the cost to society as a whole as a result of a reduced flow of new and better products and a less rapid rise in the standard of living.

Ridicule of overregulation, based, of course, on carefully researched examples, can at times be far more effective than dull statistics or general theories in getting the public concerned about the excesses of government activity. It was the widespread repetition of those "horror stories" that forced, if not shamed, OSHA into cutting back what it has admitted are "petty" regulations.[8] After all, the public did have the right to know that its tax dollars were wasted by such nonsense as setting the proper size of toilet partitions, determining how big an opening must be to be called a hole, defining when a roof is a floor, and specifying the frequency with which spittoons should be cleaned.

Figure 2, which appeared as a newspaper editorial, is an example of the effective use of the information route. Merely informing citizens that OSHA felt it necessary to issue a pamphlet telling farmers to beware of falling into manure pits accelerated the growing concern with the nonsense spewed from that federal agency.

SETTING TARGETS

If the third step of the process of improving the public environment in which business operates is raising the factual, information level, the fourth step is setting sights on some reasonable, attainable objectives. Business needs to avoid adopting obviously self-serving positions which may be expedient in the short run but which damage the central role of the enterprise system over the long run. No amount of posturing will convince broad segments of the public that business truly believes in the private enterprise system if individual companies run to Washing-

Figure 2. Dick and Jane visit the farm.

See the book.
See the little book.
See the little OSHA book.
What is OSHA?
OSHA is your government.
OSHA is the Occupational Safety and Health Administration.
OSHA helps people.
OSHA helps people to be safe.
OSHA made the little book for farmers.
What does the little book say?
This is what it says:

Be careful around the farm. . . . Hazards are one of the main causes of accidents. A hazard is anything that is dangerous.

Be careful when you are handling animals. Tired or hungry or frightened cattle can bolt and trample you. Be patient, talk softly around the cows. Don't move fast or be loud around them. If they are upset, don't go into the pen with them.

Cows are more dangerous when they have new calves. Be careful if you have to reach ·into their pen. Try not to go into the pen with them. Keep pets and children away, too.

A bawling calf can cause all the cows to be upset. If that happens, stay out of the feedlot. They could bolt and knock you down.

Always try to keep a fence between you and your cattle. Never try to handle a bull alone. Always have a helper. . . .

DON'T FALL.
Be careful that you do not fall into the manure pits. Put up signs and fences to keep people away. These pits are very dangerous. . . .

Put away tools, equipment and feed when not using them. . . . When floors are wet and slippery with manure, you could have a bad fall. . . . If your ladder is broken, do not climb it. . . .

Wear clothes that fit right.

See the farmer.
See the farmer go to the mail box.
See the farmer get the little book.
The farmer can read.
The farmer can read big words.
The farmer can read long sentences.
The farmer knows about cows.
The farmer knows about fences.
The farmer knows about manure pits.
See the farmer read the little book.
Now the farmer knows about OSHA.
See the farmer kick the mail box.
Hear the farmer say bad words.
See the farmer throw the little book.
See the farmer throw the little book into the manure pit.
See OSHA.
See OSHA write.
See OSHA print.
See OSHA throw money into the manure pit.
Say bad words about OSHA.

Reprinted with permission from the Omaha *World-Herald*, June 15, 1976.

ton to seek tariff protection or tax and credit subsidies every time they encounter some rough competition. As Professor S. Prakash Sethi of the University of Texas has put it, a "one-sided definition of free enterprise is not acceptable." [9] He has in mind support by companies of special aids to business as "bolstering the free enterprise system," while simultaneously the companies oppose pollution control as "hampering free enterprise."

One aspect of the environment that concerns business executives is that many of our citizens do not adequately understand the important role of profits as a motivating force for economic growth and efficiency—and that is a justifiable concern. But we should not forget that every student who has mastered Economics 1 knows that effective competition tends to hold down profits. Thus, the public is suspicious when the staunch advocates of free enterprise come out for those "special" types of regulations which restrict "destructive" or "excessive" competition in their specific industries. Suspicion may be warranted, therefore, in the case of "selective" or self-serving demands for regulation. Such action affects more than business credibility; it provides the rationale for all sorts of raids on the Treasury by other groups. We can recall the type of cartoon that was common at the time Congress passed the loan guarantee for Lockheed. For example, a little tailor complained, "If they can bail out Lockheed, why can't they help me?"

Conversely, business must recognize that not all critics are would-be destroyers of the private enterprise system. Most of them do want the system to work better, although they may have different views on how to go about it. There would be a much healthier debate if the business community understood that the vast majority of the critics, although surely not all, share the same ultimate objectives. That understanding would provide a common ground on which to communicate, and the process of communication would be enhanced by avoiding personal attacks and sticking to the issues. The main problem involved here—which goes back to step 3—is that many people do not understand the full impacts on the American business system of the various changes that they are urging. Literally, they see the benefits and ignore the wide range of costs. Rather than want to defeat them, the goal should be to educate people in the proper sense of the word "educate."

Business should advocate a sensible balance in government action. As a result, its views might well have an impact on the formulation of that public action. Business management, employees, and consumers share a set of values and long-term interests—a rising living standard, higher employment, and less inflation—although they may differ at times on the means of achieving those goals. There is not a single invariant set of relations among interest groups. On some issues, notably government regulation affecting jobs, business and labor may find themselves joining forces, as has been true in the automobile industry. On other occasions—as in the imposition by government of job safety standards—there may be strong differences of opinion between labor and management. And though it is naive to talk of a community of interests of business, labor, and consumers on every specific issue, it is equally inaccurate to proceed on the opposite assumption—that the relations must always be adversary.

Healthy criticism can be valuable. If the initial critics of environmental pollution had been listened to early enough, some of the overreaction which resulted in putting "zero discharge" goals into the environmental statutes might have been averted. All the participants in public policy debates believe that government should set rules for society, but that position does not justify government intervention into every activity of society.

In any event, it would be futile to advocate a return to a simpler age. Public support of environmental, safety, and similar regulations remains strong. The quarrel is not over ends, but over means; there is legitimate concern that the means used are just not effective. It is ironic that many business executives who are constantly seeking and rewarding new ideas in traditional economic matters are so widely viewed as the epitome of reactionary standpatters in matters of public policy. There is, therefore, a communications and educational task to be performed, within as well as by the business community.

In many ways, the saccharin case is a good example of what

to do as well as what to avoid. That example of overregulation has not been the occasion for urging the elimination of the Food and Drug Administration. In fact, most of the critics of the Delaney Amendment have merely urged reform, and not repeal. That example of overregulation, at least, has not led to overreaction. Similarly, public antagonism toward the compulsory interlock system on the 1974 passenger automobile led Congress to eliminate that specific requirement, but federal auto safety regulation in general continues.

Business should try to take straightforward positions on public policy issues on the assumption that should be obvious to all: Business is not a charitable institution, but an economic enterprise. Proposals for public policy that will enhance the ability of the private enterprise system to meet consumer needs should be supported. Examples range from tax changes for encouraging savings and investment to reform of onerous government regulations. Frankly, the approach does not include promoting special subsidies, such as tax shelters, which reward select groups of the society at the expense of business and individual taxpayers generally.

But business should strongly oppose measures which would adversely affect the future of the business system. Numerous examples were presented in Chapter 5; they range from the imposition of wage and price controls to breaking up the larger and more successful corporations. Such punitive measures, as was demonstrated, do not truly advance the public interest.

ENTERING THE POLICY ARENA

The fifth step requires business to attempt to alter the external environment in which it operates by entering the arena in which public policy is developed. Many business organizations do not resist the expansion of government power. They view regulation as a means of fending off "unfair" competition either at home or from abroad. Alternatively, they simply have got used to operating in an environment in which government's role is expanding or they merely are reluctant to enter a controversial area. Perhaps they hope that the critics will pick on somebody else if they maintain a low profile.

According to J. Wilson Newman, chairman of the finance committee of Dun & Bradstreet, American business holds much of its future in its own hands. As Newman states the matter, "It can stonewall the rising challenges to the corporate status quo. Or it can view those challenges as a positive force that, if directed by responsible corporate self-action, can deliver benefits to our entire society." [10]

It is neither necessary nor desirable to advocate that business take a passive role of automatically agreeing to every demand on the part of each interest group, public or private. Demands that do not make sense should be opposed—lawfully and strongly—and more sensible alternatives should be developed and presented when they are appropriate. Rather than speechify on the evils of big government or the glories of the free enterprise system, business needs to concentrate its efforts on more effectively communicating the specific impacts on the consumer of misguided proposals for excessive controls over business.

As corporate managers become more sensitive to evolving social demands, they must consider response to at least some of the public's expectations as being a normal aspect of conducting business. To the extent that the development occurs voluntarily, businesses themselves will provide an important constraint on the political pressure that social action interests can exert against them.

Nevertheless, there is no substitute for companies taking an activist attitude toward public policy matters. That includes strengthening or setting up their Washington offices. One major company compares its Washington office to an embassy: The office interprets actions of the U.S. government that have significant impact on the company and helps to formulate positions on those actions. The active approach means stronger support of trade associations working on Capitol Hill and of other legitimate ways in which business can exercise its historical right to "petition for redress of grievances." The most effective type of "lobbying" is neither the stereotyped arm-twisting nor providing financial contributions to politicians. Rather, it is the timely provision of accurate and pertinent information on the issues of public policy being debated in Congress or considered in government agencies.

Viewed in a different light, however, trade associations may be one of the most underutilized mechanisms for improving public policy. With some adaptation, those groups of companies could become the moral conscience of the business community. In the middle 1970s, for example, during the investigations of illegal corporate contributions, the individual company may have been afraid, quite properly, to respond to the public criticism of the wrongdoers, not because it approved such action, but because it feared that subsequent investigation might reveal that its own skirts were not completely clean.

Here the trade associations could have taken a stronger and more independent stand. They were in a better position to enunciate the acceptable standards of private behavior, even while acknowledging that not every person in every company was living up to those standards all the time. There surely was no shortage of reports, during the same period, of illegal actions in government agencies or labor unions. But spokesmen in those other groups, especially government, made it clear that breaking the law was not desirable behavior, but was to be condemned.

Some business firms are making more extensive use of the many channels of communication that are already available to them to raise the public awareness of political issues that affect the future of the business community. Those channels, which may currently be devoted to more traditional or operational messages, reach a wide variety of publics: employee newspapers, company magazines, and reports to shareholders; materials sent to customers, suppliers, and retired personnel; employee training and management development programs; and bulletin boards and posters on company premises.

It is in the active approach—business involvement in the public arena—that the greatest potential for improving business-government relations may lie. The role of company government relations offices, trade associations, and business in politics needs to be rethought in a more positive light.

Corporations can participate legally in a wide variety of political activities, but typically they are much more reluctant than labor unions to do so. A corporation may recommend how management, employees, and shareholders should vote. In practice, however, very few companies attempt to exercise that right to develop and communicate their views on specific candidates. Labor unions, in striking contrast, have no similar shyness. In 1976, most corporate efforts were limited to nonpartisan register-and-get-out-the-vote drives.

The management of a company has a right to state its position on public issues that affect the company's well-being, including legislative proposals before Congress. It may also communicate to its employees and stockholders information, such as voting records, on members of Congress and candidates for office. Company-sponsored programs explaining how to be effective in politics are another permissible form of political activity. A corporation can provide political education programs for employees, and it can actively promote, on a nonpartisan basis, voluntary involvement of its employees in direct political action on the employees' own time. Also, an employee may be granted a leave of absence without pay to work on a political campaign.

Critics of business involvement in politics often ignore the very substantial political contributions made by other interest groups, notably labor. For instance, in 1976 it was reported that political arms of three maritime unions had given almost $1 million to members of the House and Senate in the preceding four years. In the fall of 1974 alone, unions affiliated with the AFL-CIO—particularly the Marine Engineers Beneficial Association (MEBA)—contributed $380,000 to 154 incumbent members of the Congress who supported a bill to compel oil imports to be hauled in increasing percentages by ships with American union crews rather than by comparatively inexpensive foreign vessels. The largest union donation of $22,000 went to the senator who served as floor manager of the bill.[11]

In the 1976 national election campaign, the AFL-CIO's Committee on Political Education (COPE) reported that it spent "in the multi-millions" on top of the $2 million it devoted to its computerized election machinery. Most of labor's election efforts do not show up in official reports and hence are not subject to legal limitations. Examples include the virtual full-time assignment of union organizers and clerks to get-out-the-vote duty. In 1976, more than 10 million calls were placed from COPE's telephone banks, and 120,000 "volunteers" were involved in its car pools and doorbell ringing. As nonprofit organizations, labor unions pay low, subsidized rates on their mailings, even including campaign material.[12]

Here is how Al Barkan, the Director of COPE, evaluates his operation: "We have phone banks functioning in almost all communities of any consequence during registration and get-out-the-vote campaigns. On election day, we provide transportation to the polls for members needing it, babysitters, pollwatchers—probably more and better trained than in either political party." Mr. Barkan points out quite clearly that, "As important as funding is in politics, however, COPE's strength is people . . . the thousands of volunteers who make the COPE program go and who provide the nuts-and-bolts support services that are so crucial to winning elections." [13]

It surely seems that a double standard is being applied to those off-the-balance-sheet items of money and time. What company or trade association would dare assign its executives to full-time campaigning as part of their paid work? What companies would devote their reports to shareholders and their executives to the campaigning in which unions openly engage? To be fair, let us clearly acknowledge that nothing illegal is involved in those union activities. But given the current public sentiment toward business, companies are afraid to engage in the same type of lawful activity for fear of enraging the media and the public. Labor's political contributions simply do not receive the public attention that comparable business efforts receive.

The deck is stacked. Who can unstack it? What can be done to improve business's position in the arena of public policy? One astute and concerned observer, Irving Kristol, says "pitifully little," at least directly, because "the business of ideas, of forming opinions, of engaging in an adversary contest is not necessarily a skill within corporations." [14] Kristol urges, instead, that business mobilize independent support within the intellectual, academic, legal, and professional communities that are more likely to be effective in the opinion formation activities that take place in this nation.

There is much merit to what Kristol is saying. The Opinion Research Corporation reported in the spring of 1978 that only 30 percent of the American public believed that the ethical and moral practices of business executives were excellent or good. (In the case of advertising executives it was 29 percent.) In contrast, 56 percent of the public considered the ethics and morals of college professors and news reporters to be excellent or good.

Very frequently the statements of business executives are dismissed as too self-serving. In contrast, many efforts in the academic and research communities to improve the intellectual environment in which business operates can be useful and are worthy of substantial business support. In the words of William Simon, former Secretary of the Treasury, "The alliance between the theorists and men of action in the capitalist world is long overdue in America." Simon adds an important note of caution: "This has nothing to do with trying to govern what any individual professor teaches, nor is it an attempt to 'buy' docile professors who will teach what businessmen tell them to." [15]

Concomitantly with the support of intellectual middlemen, there is much that business can do directly. Corporate executives are most effective when they are writing or talking about matters in which they are the experts. General discourses about excessive intereference by government are not useful. But presenting simply and forcefully the factual case of the 800 bottles of soda pop a day (the equivalent of the dosage used on test animals to demonstrate carcinogenicity) has been devastating in arousing the public to oppose the proposed ban on saccharin. As noted earlier, the public outrage in turn led Congress to pass a law postponing the ban on that product. Quite clearly a strong, understandable, and accurate recitation of the facts of the matter can succeed in arousing the consumer and reaching the national consciousness. The saccharin case may well turn out to be a harbinger of things to come.

Yet Kristol is quite right in emphasizing the groups other than business that are necessarily involved in developing public policy affecting business. Those other groups are covered in the chapters that follow.

References

1. Joseph Nolan, "Protect Your Public Image with Performance," *Harvard Business Review*, March–April 1975.
2. Robert T. Quittmeyer, *The Liberation of the Consumer* (New York: Amstar Corporation, 1977), p. 4.
3. Thornton Bradshaw, "Corporate Social Reform: An Executive's Viewpoint," in S. Prakash Sethi, ed., *The Unstable Ground: Corporate Social Policy in a Dynamic Society* (Los Angeles: Melville, 1974), p. 24.
4. Frank T. Cary, *Report to Stockholders: Annual Meeting, April 24, 1978* (New York: International Business Machines Corp., 1978), p. 7.
5. Bill Abrams, "The 3-Martini Lunch Is Outclassed by Far by the $6,000 Dinner," *The Wall Street Journal*, May 5, 1978.
6. Jim Montgomery, "How a Company Jet Eases the Dog's Life of a High Executive," *The Wall Street Journal*, November 14, 1977.
7. "I.C.C. Says Carriers Bill Clients for Funds Spent in Entertaining," *The New York Times*, May 9, 1978.
8. See David Burham, "U.S. Safety Agency Being Revised to Focus on Major Work Hazards," *The New York Times*, May 20, 1977; Walter S. Mossberg, "Safety Agency Will Tighten Regulations on Health Hazards, Drop Trivial Rules," *The Wall Street Journal*, May 19, 1977.
9. S. Prakash Sethi, ed., *The Unstable Ground: Corporate Social Policy in a Dynamic Society* (Los Angeles: Melville, 1974), p. 2.
10. J. Wilson Newman, quoted in Randall Poe, "Directors: A Shark Can Help," *Across the Board*, June 1978.
11. Morton Mintz, "3 Maritime Unions Gave $1 Million in Last 4 Years," *Washington Post*, August 10, 1976.

12. A. H. Raskin, "The Labor Scene: COPE's Impact on Election Outcome," *The New York Times,* December 28, 1976.
13. Al Barkan, "The Action Started Early: U.S. Workers Have a Long Political History," *Viewpoint,* First Quarter, 1976.
14. Irving Kristol, *The Importance of Public Interest Law,* C.E.O. Luncheon on Public Interest Law, February 14, 1978 (Washington, D.C.: The National Legal Center for the Public Interest).
15. William E. Simon, *A Time for Truth* (New York: Reader's Digest Press, 1978), pp. 233, 232.

7

The Government Response: The Case for Self-Restraint

As government tries to do more, it will find it accomplishes less. That amounts to the discovery that administrative ability is not a free good, and in the absence of it the best intentioned programs can turn out to be calamities.
Senator Daniel Patrick Moynihan

SENATOR Moynihan, who is also an experienced government executive, obviously understands the limitations of government's effectiveness. However, that understanding does not seem to be widespread in the federal bureaucracy. If anything, a cavalier if not high-handed approach is characteristic of many government employees, especially those who have responsibility for dealing with the private sector. Here is a sampling of their public statements:

The director of the FDA's Bureau of Drugs explains his agency's regulation of prescription medicines: *"We do not pay any attention to the economic consequences of our decisions."* [1]

The head of the Equal Employment Opportunity Commission describes the impact of a new regulatory policy of the agency: *"It is very difficult for a company that did not start hiring yesterday—literally yesterday—not to be in violation."* [2]

A member of the Federal Trade Commission comments on a new 21-page form promulgated by the Commission: *"This will give a lot of business to a lot of lawyers."* [3]

The Department of Health, Education, and Welfare directs the school system of Oak Ridge, Tennessee, to eliminate sex discrimination in athletics: *"It also will be necessary that varsity cheerleaders cheer equally for both boys' and girls' varsity teams."* [4]

The presiding officer of the FTC proceeding on food advertising justifies the agency's proposed intervention: *"People often eat for the wrong reasons."* [5]

As pointed out at the end of the preceding chapter, business itself cannot handle all of the serious problems that arise in the public policy arena. There is, of course, a central role for government. But the initial task that the public sector needs to undertake—and it will permeate all the proposals that follow—is a variation of step 3, providing information, which was described in Chapter 6: Government needs to improve greatly its understanding of the multifarious impacts on business that flow from public policies. That is, government officials at all levels should make greater efforts to inform themselves on what is happening in the rest of the economy as a result of government intervention and temper their actions in the light of that better information.

For example, Congress has never passed a law to increase unemployment or reduce business productivity, to inhibit capital formation, or to slow the rate of innovation. Yet, as we have seen, those adverse consequences frequently flow from government intervention in business. In large part, the private sector is faced with government officials who have never worked in a private company and who simply may not understand the impact of their actions on business or the economy. It is a question not of malice or venality, but of lack of understanding.

As might be expected, most of the criticism of the practice of government regulation, both by those who want more and those who want less, is aimed at the regulators who carry out the government programs. Although the regulators are indeed fair targets in many instances, the basic culprits are often the members of Congress who do not review and update the mass of legislation that they place on the statute books and who currently have little incentive to do so. In the final analysis, each regulation is promulgated under the authority provided by some law that is still in existence. The objectionable regulation may simply be stipulated by a statute which is out of date or one which was drawn up with inadequate attention to the full consequences.

That the conclusion is widely shared can be seen by the letter a Treasury Department employee of long standing felt impelled to write to a newspaper editor in the summer of 1978: "But consider, if you will, the mass of poorly designed, ill-focused legislation the bureaucrat has to administer. . . . No band of angels, much less mere human beings, could cope with the complexities or the schizophrenic nature of these programs." [6]

An insight into the shortcomings of the congressional decision-making process was furnished by the unfortunate incident of the "hour breather." When Congress was drafting the Coal Mine Health and Safety Act of 1969, it heard testimony about a German device (the Auer breather) that provided coal miners with a badly needed half-hour oxygen supply in case of fire. Wanting to insure that the important advance was available to American miners, it ordered the Bureau of Mines to develop such a portable oxygen breather. Unfortunately, something got garbled in the process and the law stipulates an *hour* breather. It took the Bureau almost a decade to meet that unnecessarily stringent requirement, during which time more than 100 miners died of asphyxiation. [7]

ENHANCING THE EFFECTIVENESS OF GOVERNMENT

There is a strong temptation on the part of the defenders of the status quo in public policy to attack all suggestions for reform as mere attempts to lessen the role of government per se. There is a positive thrust, however, to the reforms suggested here: Government should do well the important tasks that it is assigned to perform. The public welfare is not served by an incompetent bureaucracy that is an attractive and vulnerable target for critics.

As Bayless Manning has pointed out, it is not just private enterprise that is regulated into slow motion. Government agencies often find themselves immobilized by their own regulations and stymied by the regulations of other government agencies; proliferation of regulatory requirements and prerequisite clearances is making it extremely difficult, if not impossible, for society to respond to the very social problems to which so many of the recent statutes and rules are addressed.[8]

Almost anyone who has been involved in the operation of the federal government comes away with a basic feeling of frustration. Despite the vast amount of resources expended, it is extremely difficult to get anything accomplished, especially anything that is new or different, except in a generally perceived period of crisis. New mechanisms and new organizations have a role in developing better government priorities and policies, yet there is something far more basic that is absent in most discussions of the subject: However high the quality and amount of resources being devoted to carrying out government programs, the resources are far exceeded by the multiplicity of the tasks imposed by Congress. The issue that fact raises is a very practical one. On an increasing scale, Congress has either imposed directly or required the bureaucracy to establish a truly staggering array of detail to accompany each of the regulatory, tax, and expenditure activities. The attempt by governments to direct private action so completely is often, quite simply, self-defeating.

The overexpansion of federal responsibilities is not limited to business; it extends to other parts of the private sector and to the public sector as well. Here is how the Advisory Commission on Intergovernmental Relations sees the problems of federal regulation from the viewpoint of states and localities receiving federal grants in aid:

Government-wide requirements—not directly germane to the purpose of the grants but intended to advance some other national objective—were now new sources of delays, confusion, costs, and controversy. . . . Required reports sometimes involved thousands of pages, and grant recipients were faced with conflicting standards.[9]

The same problem was dealt with by the president of Harvard University who devoted *all* of his report for 1974–1975 to the problem of federal regulation and ancillary "requirements of Byzantine complexity." One paragraph of that report is especially noteworthy:

When educators grumble about excessive regulation or criticize the costs of complying with federal law, their complaints must seem familiar to every businessman who has ever experienced the travails of government intervention. In many ways, the complaints *are* similar.

There are many reasons why policy makers need to be concerned about the exhaustive detail and trivia in government activities. It is all well and good to talk about new priorities and new policies, but try serving in the White House in an incoming administration and try getting the bureaucracy to do something new or different. It becomes a truly herculean task, and not because of the desire of the civil service to frustrate the will of a new set of political appointees. Rather, the existing governmental machinery is so busy trying to carry on the staggering array of responsibilities which the Congress already has assigned to it that it cannot readily accommodate itself to a new and therefore increased workload. The traditional response—to set up yet another government agency—clearly results in a scale of federal operations far beyond any effective span of control.

That point has been made by many experienced observers. It was perhaps voiced most forcefully by William Carey, former assistant director of the U.S. Bureau of the Budget:

There is no way that government can pile on an infinitely growing pyramid of roles and responsibilities without coming to a breaking point. . . . Government will be obliged to shed unmanageable operational activities and bureaucracies—to lighten its own bulk.[10]

We need to begin with a very simple idea, but one that is likely to be very difficult to carry out. Reordering priorities consists of two parts. The first, which is the easier and the more interesting, is to identify the new and higher priorities which are to receive larger shares of our resources and attention. The current concern with increasing the domestic supply of energy is a good example.

But the process of reordering priorities is not finished until the second part has been completed—identifying the older and lower priorities which are to receive smaller shares of our resources and attention. That is by far the more neglected but more difficult part of the task. Thus, in effect, the advice is a variant of an old refrain, "Don't just stand there, undo something." That is hardly a plea for dismantling the federal establishment, but reducing or eliminating the excessive detail is an essential step in making available to government decision makers the necessary time and money that can be devoted to new and better public undertakings.

To obtain some perspective on the potential for weeding out low-priority government activities, it is useful to flip through just one issue of a standard government document, the *Federal Register,* which contains the rules and regulations promulgated by federal agencies. The January 16, 1976, issue is dominated by 94 pages of tables which contain the minimum wage rates for federal and federally assisted construction established by the Secretary of Labor under the Davis-Bacon Act.

Of the remainder of the January 16 *Register,* a major item relates to the orange juice standards of the Food and Drug Administration. The section ranges from the types of equipment which are deemed acceptable to measure the color of orange juice to the number of points required (36 to 40) for canned orange juice to qualify as being of "good color." That fascinating portion of the *Register* is followed by lemon regulation 22, which restricts the number of lemons that may be shipped from California and Arizona during the period January 18–24. Another FDA regulation then describes the handling of dried prunes.

Several of the other items in the January 16 *Register* may be of somewhat greater importance. They deal with standards on school bus brakes, procedures for making rural housing loans, advertising for eyeglasses, subsidies for local railroad service, and the amount of public notice that must be given if a drawbridge is required to be open. But obviously, not all of the items in the January 16 *Register* necessarily impress the casual reader as being the matters of high national policy that the Founding Fathers presumably had in mind in forming "a more perfect union."

The emphasis in any reform effort should be not on how much more government can do but on which tasks government should undertake and on how those important tasks can be performed in a satisfactory manner. After all, as Hubert Humphrey, the enthusiastic advocate of government action, was moved to state, "The government goes around willy-nilly making decisions of consequence. . . . The manner in which we are presently utilizing government resources and government agencies is a haphazard, helter-skelter enterprise." [11]

The present time is one in which public disenchantment with government is growing rapidly. The thrust of the approach suggested here is to respond constructively to that disenchantment by forcing government to act more sensibly and reasonably. The result would be to shore up the badly needed public faith in government and to enlist public support for the things that government does do. The government badly needs to get its own house in order so as to avoid the inevitable criticism, "Physician, heal thyself."

MOVING TOWARD A SOLUTION

The corporation is, of course, a creature of the state. In theory —although perhaps not in practice—government can impose on business an endless array of social responsibilities. Our concern here, and government's as well, is not with the welfare of the corporation as such—after all, who can get truly excited about an organizational form? Rather, the proper concern is with the ability of the corporation to serve society's purposes. There are those who are overly impressed with the might of the large corporations. One "corporate activist" writes, "Corporations are powerful; they are where the action is. . . . Corporate leaders . . . don't suffer from dirty air or crowded living conditions or traffic jams. . . . For whatever reason, the corporation is simply extremely powerful and may well be the most powerful single institution in this country." [12]

To this corporate activist and to his equally excitable colleagues, we must point out that the power of the largest private company dwindles into insignificance when compared with that of government. No business possesses the authority to levy a tax or throw a citizen into jail—or free its senior executives from traffic jams.

In any event, restraint is needed in the exercise of the great power of government over business—especially in imposing social burdens on business. Those social burdens interfere with the corporation's ability to perform its basic job for society: producing goods and services and creating jobs and income in the process. The frequently made point that business cannot be divorced from the society in which it operates is, of course, valid. But that notion needs to be tempered by the realization that there are effective limits to the ability of the business firm to take on a host of ancillary responsibilities. Many of those who urge business to take on an endless array of social burdens simply have not stopped to consider the adverse impacts of such well-intentioned actions.

In general terms, of course, government decision makers often do acknowledge the problem. Senator Daniel Inouye made the point in a statement to a congressional committee studying corporate rights and responsibilities:

> Even though the corporation—both global and domestic—is an institution with enormous economic, political, and social influence, we must avoid the temptation of imposing so many constraints on it so as to prevent it from working properly. [13]

In a similar vein, John Dunlop, when he was Secretary of Labor, wrote:

It is an open question as to how many regulations a business, particularly one of small or medium size, can absorb. . . . The country needs to acquire a more realistic understanding of the limits to the degree to which social change can be brought through legal compulsion. . . . Government has more regulation on its plate than it can handle.[14]

The difficulty, of courses, is in moving from general statements to specific actions that will produce change. By drawing on the materials in Chapter 4, let us try to develop a constructive approach to reforming the existing structure of government regulation of business.

REFORM OF REGULATION

The basic task of government in the regulatory reform area is not to be preoccupied with either technical measurements of benefits and costs or administrative procedures. Instead, the federal government leadership—in Congress, the White House, and the executive agencies—needs to take a fundamentally different *view* of the regulatory mechanism than it does now. Rather than rely on regulation to control in detail every facet of private behavior, the regulatory device needs to be seen as a very powerful tool to be used reluctantly and with great care and discretion. A good deal of judgment is required in sorting out the hazards that are important to regulate from the lesser kinds of hazard that, in Charles L. Schultze's terms, can best be dealt with by "the normal prudence of consumers, workers, and business firms." [15]

But, to be quite blunt, achievement of that worthy goal has been, and will continue to be, impeded because of lack of information on the part of government and its regulators. Allen Ferguson, the head of the Public Interest Economics Foundation, has described an important part of the problem: "The government has little reliable knowledge of consumer (voter) preferences, of consumers' perception of the benefit to them of current programs, or of their expected gains or losses from proposed actions." [16]

To correct this sorry situation, a new way of looking at the microeconomic effects of government programs is needed. A parallel can be drawn with general or macroeconomic policy, in which important and at times conflicting objectives are recognized simultaneously. Attempts at reconciliation are made among such factors as economic growth, employment, income distribution, and price stability. At the programmatic or microeconomic level, it is also necessary to reconcile the goals of specific government programs with other important national objectives, which are not now *in practice* the concern of many of those agencies. In part, the reconciliation needs to be made at the most basic stages of the governmental process—when the President proposes and Congress enacts a new regulatory program.

One device for broadening the horizons of government policy makers and administrators is the economic impact statement (see Chapter 4). It would be similar to the well-known environmental impact statement. Policy makers should be required to consider the costs and other adverse effects as well as the benefits of their actions. In that economic way of looking at public policy, no single objective is elevated to absolute, overriding priority. To be sure, it is necessary to avoid setting up the type of institutionalized paper-shuffling operation that characterized the planning-programming-budgeting effort of the mid-1960s and the zero-based budgeting approach of more recent years. Top management in government must focus on key areas of decision making and thus avoid the type of situation that Norman Macrae satirized in describing the work of the Office of Technology Assessment: "If you invent a better mousetrap in America, then this Committee . . . is authorized to inquire whether this might be environmentally unfair to mice." [17]

Applying economic analysis to regulation is not a novel idea. In November 1974, President Gerald Ford instructed the federal agencies under his jurisdiction to examine the effects of major regulatory actions on costs, productivity, employment, and other economic factors. With modifications, that approach has been continued under President Carter. This first step, however, is subject to several shortcomings.

First, many of the key regulatory agencies—ranging from the Consumer Product Safety Commission to the Federal Trade

Commission—are so-called independent agencies, which are beyond the President's jurisdiction in these matters. Second, the agencies covered by the executive order are required only to examine the economic aspects of their actions. The weight they give those economic factors remains in their discretion—to the extent that congressional statutes permit them to give any consideration to economic influences at all.

Within those constraints, the Council on Wage and Price Stability has intervened in many cases of proposed regulation to offer its analyses of the benefits and costs of a proposed action. The regulatory agencies have rarely welcomed that advice from another federal agency, but the publicity given some of the Council's analyses may have at times provided a deterrent to the adoption of the extreme ideas of the personnel of regulatory agencies.

A broader approach is warranted, one with a strong legislative mandate. In the fashion of the environmental impact statements (but hopefully without as much of the trivia), Congress should require each regulatory agency to assess the impact of its proposed actions on society as a whole, and particularly on the economy. Some type of quantitative analysis, such as benefit/cost estimation, may have a useful role in that process. But policy formation needs to proceed beyond merely another set of so-called economic impact statements.

First of all, the costs and the benefits of government actions should be more than examined; they should be weighed one against the other. In the process, the actual or proposed regulations that generate excessive costs should be modified or eliminated. Government agencies do not now have any incentive to be concerned with the costs they impose on the economy. So the analysis needs to go beyond the direct impact on price and include the relations to employment, productivity, capital formation, and innovation. That approach to government policy involves the setting of analytical and measurement standards for government regulatory agencies by a unit not itself involved in conducting regulatory programs, such as the General Accounting Office or the Office of Management and Budget. The "arms-length relationship" is needed to insure uniformity in the measurement of benefits, costs, and other effects. Such standards would reduce the temptation of individual regulatory agencies to present self-serving justifications of existing activities, since the agencies would then be operating in a new economic framework.

Attention therefore needs to be given to the role of the budget process in managing regulation. Regulatory agencies currently have little reason to devote their limited budgets to the pursuit of economically efficient regulation. They must be forced to do so via the budget process. When an agency's regulations generate more costs than benefits, its budget for the coming year should be reduced because, clearly, not all of its activities are worthwhile. Budget reviewers, be they examiners in the executive branch or committee staffs in the legislature, face the perennial question of how to measure the effectiveness of an agency that does not provide marketable outputs. The traditional response is to concentrate on the inputs utilized (as, for example, workload statistics), which tends to reward bureaucratic routine. Benefit/cost analysis and cost-effectiveness analysis (which helps to identify the least-cost solutions), can provide useful alternative approaches for allocating public resources.

Because the requested appropriations for the regulatory agencies are relatively small portions of the government's budget, limited attention has been given to those activities in the budget process. In view of the large costs that regulations often impose on society as a whole (those hidden taxes shifted to the private sector), greater attention to the reviews of the appropriation requests for regulatory programs is warranted.

It is, in short, important to build into the governmental processes incentives that would encourage government officials to give greater weight to the costs and other side effects generated by the actions that they take. Limiting new regulations to instances in which it can be demonstrated that net benefits accrue to society as a whole is one such device. The result would be not an absence of new regulation, but useful regulation which is more likely to meet the goals desired by the nation without incurring either waste or detrimental side effects.

Opportunities for sensibly economizing on costs in achieving important regulatory objectives are numerous. A case in point is provided by the proposed job safety standards for exposure to lead in the workplace. OSHA would require smelters, battery manufacturers, and other firms to install engineering controls that reduce by half the maximum exposure level from the present 200 micrograms of lead per cubic meter of air to 100 micrograms. The U.S. Council on Wage and Price Stability has estimated that meeting the proposed standards could cost the industries affected —and ultimately consumers—over $300 million a year. The Council urges that OSHA allow each company to use the most efficient way to achieve the new standard, whether that requires costly engineering controls or some other method.

Intensive employee training might be one of those alternate methods if a study in the United Kingdom can serve as a guide. According to a report in the *British Journal of Industrial Medicine,* the lead exposures of employees doing almost identical jobs differed by ratios of up to four to one. That was totally attributed to personal differences in working habits.[18] In the United States, the National Safety Council estimates that 75 to 85 percent of industrial accidents are caused by persons who lack "safety consciousness."

The poet, not given to pragmatism, may tell us that "high Heaven rejects the lore/Of nicely-calculated less or more." [19] But the practical necessities of everyday life compel us to realize that resources used in one direction without a useful result just are not available for other and possibly more productive purposes— to the detriment of society's total welfare, at least by earthly considerations. And if considerations of national economic welfare do not arouse government decision makers to change their ways, an appeal to their own self-interest should. Clearly, citizen disenchantment with government intervention in private matters is growing rapidly. Those who are truly concerned with maintaining public support for programs of social regulation should reflect carefully on the message from Charles L. Schultze, former senior fellow at the Brookings Institution and currently chairman of the Council of Economic Advisers in the Carter administration:

> The rash of new regulatory mechanisms established in recent years—for pollution control, energy conservation, industrial health and safety, consumer-product quality and safety, and the like—have generated a backlash of resentment against excessive red tape and bureaucratic control.[20]

That often negative public reaction to the new wave of regulation is supported by Dr. Schultze's own evaluation:

> Efforts to improve the environment . . . are unnecessarily expensive and increasingly bogged down in Rube Goldberg regulations. . . . Even the sympathetic observer finds it hard to recognize many of the [industrial safety] regulations as anything but *absurdities*.[21]

Every once in a while, the bureaucracy does move and gives us hope that substantial improvement is possible. For example, in the early fall of 1978, the FDA applied some sensible risk/benefit analysis in its approach to nitrites. Under the zero-risk approach of the Delaney Amendment, the FDA could have banned nitrites as a carcinogenic food additive. It did not do so because the chemical does far more good than harm—by reducing the hazard of botulism, a deadly poison. Very sensibly, the agency relied on an information strategy, urging the public to reduce where possible its use of this complex substance.

GUIDING PRINCIPLES FOR GOVERNMENT OFFICIALS

On the basis of this and earlier chapters, we may be able to develop some useful principles to guide legislators and regulators to more sensible approaches in their dealings with the private sector.

Private Choice

Consumers do not wish the government to protect them against every conceivable hazard. Even in the highly emotional area of cancer, a 1978 survey by Cambridge Reports, Inc. revealed that most Americans prefer to make their own decisions regarding the benefits or risks of using substances suspected of being carcinogenic (cancer-causing). Of the sample, 66 percent favored allowing individuals to make their own risk/benefit decisions compared with 22 percent who favored the federal government banning such substances. A very large percentage of those interviewed, 82 percent, preferred information on packages "in plain English" outlining the possible danger involved in the use of that product. Then, they said, they could make their own decisions intelligently.[22]

The Circuit Court for the District of Columbia made that point in a 1978 decision siding with the plaintiff who appealed a standard of the Consumer Product Safety Commission: "If consumers have accurate information, and still choose to incur the risk, then their judgment may well be reasonable." [23] According to Professor Yale Brozen of the University of Chicago, "Those who call themselves consumer advocates passionately try to force into products features not wanted by all consumers." Brozen states that businesses resist those requirements not because they are interested in producing useless or unsafe products, but because the required features are not desired by *all* customers.[24] The individual, for example, may choose to enhance his or her safety by spending money on smoke detectors for the home rather than on air bags for a car. Clearly, the economic approach advocated here does not quarrel at all with the social objective of a safer environment. But it suggests ways that are likely to work far better than the command-and-control mechanisms which now dominate public policy.

The importance of allowing proper scope for individual choice is demonstrated by the treatment for Rocky Mountain spotted fever. It turns out that the drug that cures the disease causes fatal anemia in one out of every 10,000 people who use it. But the disease itself will kill approximately eight out of every ten people who contract it.[25] Clearly, this is an instance in which the individual patient and his or her physician can and should make the informed choice.

The beta-blocker drugs developed for heart patients reveal the dilemma that arises when the choice is limited by the government. Certain types of beta-blockers have not been approved for general use in the United States because long-term tests on rodents reveal toxicity, including carcinogenicity. One prospective user, who seriously considered emigrating to Europe (where such drugs are more readily available), responded to the situation with some anguish: "I am over 50. I have had two coronary bypass operations. I have severe angina. I don't give a damn about what happens to the rats." [26]

Thus, the first guiding principle for government officials can be phrased as follows:

1. The individual should have maximum opportunity for personal choice.

Stress on Information and Incentives

Two corollaries of the first principle can be developed. The first follows directly from the notion of consumer choice. The second, drawing on the analysis in earlier chapters, requires a search for least-cost solutions that would enhance the effectiveness of private sector response to government policy:

2. Whenever possible, the government should provide information rather than commands.

3. Whenever possible, the government should provide incentives rather than directives.

Professor Lester Lave of Carnegie-Mellon University contends that the primary deficiency in current government regulation is in the area of collecting data, performing analyses, sponsoring research, and disseminating the information gained. Providing such information would help consumers, of course. But it could play a major role in enabling manufacturers to improve their products voluntarily.[27]

Business as the Fall Guy

Business is, of course, an inviting target for criticism because of its size and visibility, yet many of the problems with which public policy makers deal arise from shortcomings in other parts of society. For example, when the Nassau-Suffolk Regional Planning Board investigated the environmental problems in those suburban counties in the New York metropolitan area, it found that lawn fertilizer—not industrial discharges—was the leading contributor of nitrates in the area's groundwater. Similarly, the principal source of pollutants in the area's Great South Bay, the most productive natural clam producer in the world, was not from business operations, but from dog feces.[28]

Another example arises in the field of consumer product regulation. In its June 1978 "Memo to Consumers," the Consumer Product Safety Commission reports that, since 1973, bicycles have held first place on the Consumer Product Hazard Index, which lists products associated with the most numerous and severe injuries. However, later on the same article tells about a commission employee who rides his own bike five miles to work and back home each day. According to the employee, most of the bicycle-related injuries treated in hospital emergency rooms each year are caused not by problems with bicycles, but by problems with the user and road traffic. Still, the headline for the article reads, "Bicycles Still No. 1 on CPSC Hazard Index." Similarly, in the case of regulating the noise from a consumer product—motorcycles—once again the government (EPA) has taken action against the manufacturer, even though most of the problem arises from modifications to the vehicle exhaust system made by the owners.

A fourth guideline thus should deal with restraining the tendency to look toward the business system for the source of all that ails our society:

4. Good public policy should avoid the simplistic notion that all shortcomings originate in business.

"Do As I Say"

Another point that needs to be made relates to equity. Far too often, government is in a position to tell private citizens and business people, "Do as I say, not as I do." Water pollution provides a cogent example. By mid-1977, an impressive 3,600 out of 4,000 major industrial polluters had met cleanup deadlines. But only 4,150 of the nation's 12,500 municipalities met their deadlines.[29]

In addition, federal installations are among the worst polluters. In June 1977 the Environmental Protection Agency reported which industries had complied with a water cleanup deadline, but it failed to disclose that the biggest polluter was the U.S. government. By conservative estimates, 25 percent of all federal facilities in the country failed to comply with regulations intended to develop and maintain clean water. The list of federal polluters included Quantico Marine Base, the Navy Yard in Washington, Forts Lee and Belvoir in Virginia, Fort Benning in Georgia, Yosemite National Park, power plants in Wyoming and South Carolina, 14 of 38 federal facilities in Illinois, and 92 of 185 facilities in areas of the Midwest. By the government's own reports, 90 percent of private industry had, by comparison, complied with the deadline at a cost of untold billions of dollars. None of the government installations, however, were threatened with lawsuits or other government sanctions.[30]

The EPA's experience is by no means unusual. OSHA provides another outrageous example. The Supreme Court ruled in 1978 that warrants are required before OSHA makes its inspection of the workplace. Nevertheless, OSHA continues to conduct inspections in the same manner it always has: It appears at places of employment without notice and without warrants. OSHA's expectation is that most employers will waive their constitutional rights and allow its inspectors onto their premises without court authorization, presumably to avoid irritating a powerful government agency that has the power to levy large fines on private employers.

The attitude of OSHA toward federal agencies is markedly different. In the case of the Navy, for example, Admiral Hyman Rickover refuses to let OSHA inspectors on the premises, and OSHA does not attempt to force the issue by obtaining warrants to enable it to make the inspections. Recent investigations by the General Accounting Office reveal substantial health hazards in Navy shipyards such as prolonged exposure to asbestos, which can cause lung cancer. Overall, sick pay, lost time, and damage to equipment resulting from job-related sickness and injuries of federal workers were estimated at $5 billion in 1977.[31]

Similar hypocrisy is evident at state and local levels of government. In St. Louis, an inspection of the fire department's headquarters revealed "extremely hazardous" violations of the city's building and fire prevention codes. The violations included blocked fire exits, improper storage of flammable liquids, and a general lack of exits.[32] Surely, government needs to avoid following a double standard. Thus another guideline for regulations should be:

5. *Government should set an example and not put itself above the law.*

Priority and Government Power

In all their dealings with individuals and business firms, government agencies should focus on the serious and important areas in which the need for intervention is clear. Perhaps every government official should have stamped on his or her T-shirt the old Latin legal maxim: "De minimis non curat lex" (the law is not concerned with trifles). This maxim may have been violated when a topless/bottomless nightclub waitress who was seven months pregnant complained that she had been laid off because of her condition. The Colorado Civil Rights Commission dutifully scheduled a hearing for this complaint on sex discrimination!

The trivia encountered in government are not, of course, limited to dealings with the private sector; they are evident in the public sector as well. The snail darter has become a *cause celebre*. Construction of a $119 million dam being built by the Tennessee Valley Authority was halted by the Supreme Court because a new species of darter—the one hundred sixteenth— was discovered during the construction period in the area that would be affected by the dam. The absolute rigidity of the Endangered Species Act, which was the basis for the Court's decision, is reminiscent of that of the Delaney Amendment affecting food additives, discussed in an earlier chapter. In this case, however, the regulatory legislation seems to be more than merely rigid. It seems to reverse the Biblical injunction to man to "have dominion over the fish of the sea" (Genesis 1:28).

Whether government concern is for a healthier environment or safer products, policy makers must realize that not all hazards are equal. Government policy needs to distinguish between hidden and visible hazards, voluntary and involuntary hazards, easily avoidable and hard-to-avoid hazards, remote and commonplace hazards, and negligible and severe hazards. Such distinctions would help to focus government actions on the important segments of private activity which government can constructively affect.

Without repeating the many instances of silliness in government regulations covered in earlier chapters, the sixth guideline should be:

6. *The vast power of government should not be aimed at trivia.*

Looking Down the Road

Finally, government needs to be cognizant of the long-term implications of its actions. As pointed out in an article in *Fortune,* the data demonstrate a relation between a nation's health and the strength of its economy.[33] In the process of trying to reduce health and safety hazards to very low levels, regulation could inflict grave damage not only on the health of the economy but ultimately on the health of the citizenry as well. Clearly, government decision makers need to be concerned with the future impacts of their current actions.

The shifting concerns of the Consumer Product Safety Commission in the well-known Tris chemical case provide, unfortunately, a cogent example. First, the agency required manufacturers of children's sleepwear to make the fabric (primarily polyester) flame-resistant. The major chemical used was 2,3-dibromopropyl (Tris). But after the specially treated garments were in widespread use among children up to the age of 12, the government agency found that Tris was a potential source of cancer, either when ingested or when absorbed through the skin. The CPSC believed that the cancer hazard was greater than the fire hazard, and it subsequently banned the sale of children's sleepwear containing Tris.

The story does not end there, however. The ban sparked a storm of protest from clothing manufacturers and retail stores, who argued that they often had no way to determine what chemicals the manufacturers of the sleepwear cloth were using and who maintained that they were bearing an unfair economic burden. The companies that produced and sold most of the pajamas were, by and large, small firms that faced great difficulty in absorbing the large financial losses involved. A circuit court in Virginia finally overturned the CPSC ban, declaring that the Commission had acted arbitrarily and capriciously in banning only the sale of Tris-treated garments and not the use of the chemical as well. The CPSC later revised and cut back many of its standards for flame-resistant sleepwear.[34] In short, though the case is far more complicated than it would appear here, this brief summary indicates the serious problems that emerge when powerful government agencies—whose mandates have the power of law—shoot from the hip in issuing regulations.

The highly publicized labor relations case involving J. P. Stevens, the textile company, further illustrates government's tendency to abuse its power. To be sure, there were instances in this case when individual members of management overstepped the bounds of good judgment and, apparently, the law. For example, within two days after their names were posted as union members, three employees of the company were fired. It is appropriate that the National Labor Relations Board acted on that matter.

But another incident of "unfair labor practices" was of a different nature. It involved a supervisor at J. P. Stevens who merely asked a question of two employees who were walking through a company factory drumming up attendance at a speech by a union organizer. The supervisor's query was ruled to be a "gratuitous, condescending, and unjustified remark" and was judged to be a coercive act. The offending question was, "Can I help you?" It is unnerving, therefore, to contemplate the long-term implication of this government action. Does the National Labor Relations Board intend that every remark by any supervisor to any employee must be "justified" and that none can be "gratuitous" or "condescending" as determined by a federal agency? [35]

Clearly, the NLRB is concerned with following its congressional mandate to provide workers with opportunities to decide freely on whether they want to join unions. But the agency appears to have overlooked the longer-term implications of its actions in the J. P. Stevens case. By so severely restricting members of management in their ability to express themselves to employees, the federal agency ultimately limits their freedom of speech. (That, incidentally, is a freedom guaranteed by the First Amendment of the U.S. Constitution.) Consequently, we can derive from cases such as this one the seventh and final guideline for government officials:

7. Government should learn that its decisions often can produce long-term and unexpected consequences.

The large-scale and often rigid nature of government intervention in business is more than a question of costs and other immediate side effects. It is a matter of eroding society's vital capacity to adapt to and digest change—an essential characteristic for survival and growth.

We see, then, that government regulation of business has become more than merely costly or inconvenient. It has become a mode of operation that has wide-ranging and often unforeseeable consequences on American society as a whole. For that reason alone, perhaps government ought to take heed in some fashion of guidelines such as those just presented. The cavalier and high-handed approach of many government officials—so clearly illustrated at the start of this chapter—must not persist. Instead, attitudes and policies formed by the best information about, and the greatest understanding of, the nature of regulatory actions in their widest scope should prevail.

Since the opening of this chapter contained a quotation from a specific government official, J. Richard Crout, it might be appropriate to end with another quotation from the same official.

In a paper called "The Nature of Regulatory Choices," Dr. Crout addressed the issues with which this chapter is concerned, and summarized the dilemma which both government and the society for which it operates now face: "In the business of regulation, there are few clear-cut choices between vice and virtue. There are only hard compromises among competing desirable goals." [36] An enlightened public opinion is necessary to force government decision makers to make those hard choices.

References

1. J. Richard Crout, in Robert Helms, ed., *Drug Development and Marketing* (Washington, D.C.: American Enterprise Institute, 1975), p. 197.
2. Editorial in the *Indianapolis News,* March 18, 1978. The statement is not taken out of context. The head of the EEOC appears to have a penchant for strong language. She offered the following advice at a convention of the NAACP soon after the Bakke decision on affirmative action programs: "To those who have rolled out the coffins for affirmative action, let us send them back empty. . . . The Bakke decision is not a call to lay down your arms. It is a challenge to choose your weapons." "Major Corporations Warned by U.S. That They Must Hire Blacks," *St. Louis Post-Dispatch,* July 6, 1978.
3. "Federal Trade Group Wants Notification of Proposed Mergers," *St. Louis Post-Dispatch,* February 15, 1978.
4. Quoted by George F. Will, "HEW Is Ludicrous—But Not Funny," *St. Louis Globe-Democrat,* March 4, 1978.
5. William D. Dixon, in "FTC Staff Report States Calorie Disclosure Vital in Energy-Claiming Ads," *NSDA Bulletin,* National Soft Drink Association, April 10, 1978.
6. Edward P. Snyder, "What Bureaucrats Have to Cope With," *The New York Times,* June 13, 1978.
7. Ben A. Franklin, "Confusion and a 10-Year Task," *The New York Times,* July 7, 1978.
8. Bayless Manning, "Hyperlexis: Our National Disease," *Northwestern University Law Review,* January–February 1977.
9. Advisory Commission on Intergovernmental Relations, *Categorical*

Grants: Their Role and Design (Washington, D.C.: GPO, 1978), p. 40.

10. William D. Carey, "New Perspectives on Governance," in The Conference Board, *Challenge to Leadership* (New York: Free Press, 1973), pp. 68–69.

11. Hubert Humphrey, "Planning Economic Policy: An Interview with Hubert H. Humphrey," *Challenge*, March–April 1975.

12. Philip W. Moore, "Corporate Social Responsibility: An Activist's Viewpoint," in S. Prakash Sethi, ed., *The Unstable Ground: Corporate Social Policy in a Dynamic Society* (Los Angeles: Melville, 1974), p. 48.

13. Senator Daniel Inouye, U.S. Senate, Committee on Commerce, *Corporate Rights and Responsibilities* (Washington, D.C.: GPO, 1975), p. 8.

14. John T. Dunlop, "The Limits of Legal Compulsion," in Arthur Elkins and Dennis W. Callaghan, eds., *A Managerial Odyssey: Problems in Business and Its Environment* (Reading, Mass.: Addison-Wesley, 1978), pp. 374, 375.

15. Henry Owen and Charles L. Schultze, "Introduction," *Setting National Priorities: The Next Ten Years* (Washington, D.C.: Brookings Institution, 1976), p. 10.

16. Allen R. Ferguson, "Reforming Regulations in the Public Interest," *Public Interest Economics*, January 1978.

17. Norman Macrae, *America's Third Century* (New York: Harcourt Brace Jovanovich, 1976), p. 19.

18. M. K. Williams, E. King, and Joan Walford, "An Investigation of Lead Absorption in an Electric Accumulator Factory with the Use of Personal Samples," *British Journal of Industrial Medicine*, No. 26 (1969).

19. William Wordsworth, "Ecclesiastical Sonnets," III.43.

20. Charles L. Schultze, *The Public Use of Private Interest* (Washington, D.C.: Brookings Institution, 1977), p. 2.

21. Ibid., p. 4.

22. "Most Citizens Want to Make Own Cancer Risk Decisions, Survey Finds," *NSDA Bulletin*, June 19, 1976.

23. Circuit Court for the District of Columbia, *Aqua Slide 'N Dive Corporation v. The Consumer Product Safety Commission* (1978).

24. Yale Brozen et al., *Can the Market Sustain an Ethic?* (Chicago: University of Chicago, 1978), pp. 16–17.

25. *Monsanto Speaks Up About Chemicals* (St. Louis: Monsanto Co., 1977), p. 5.
26. Gerald D. Laubach, speech before the Pharmaceutical Manufacturers Association, Boca Raton, Florida, April 5, 1978.
27. Lester B. Lave, "Risk, Safety, and the Role of Government," in *Perspectives on Benefit-Risk Decision Making* (Washington, D.C.: National Academy of Engineering, 1972), p. 107.
28. Frances Cerra, "Mr. and Mrs. America and All That Slips to Sea," *The New York Times,* June 25, 1978.
29. Gladwin Hill, "Environmental Lag Is Reported for 1977," *The New York Times,* February 4, 1978.
30. William H. Jones, "When Will Federal Government Clean Up Its Act?" *Washington Post,* October 6, 1977.
31. "Labor Unit Won't Alter Inspection Policy Despite High Court Requiring Warrants," *The Wall Street Journal,* June 1, 1978; Philip Shabecoff, "U.S. Agencies Lagging in Work Safeguards," *The New York Times,* June 22, 1978; "Safety Checks for Everybody but Uncle Sam," *Chicago Sun-Times,* June 23, 1978.
32. "City Fire Code—For Others Only," *St. Louis Globe-Democrat,* March 4, 1978.
33. Tom Alexander, "OSHA's Ill-Conceived Crusade Against Cancer," *Fortune,* July 3, 1978.
34. See Nadine Brozan, "U.S. Bans a Flame-Retardant Used in Children's Sleepwear," *The New York Times,* April 8, 1977; Austin Scott, "Curbs Eased on Flammable Sleepwear," *Washington Post,* August 16, 1977.
35. Walter Guzzardi, Jr., "How the Union Got the Upper Hand on J. P. Stevens," *Fortune,* June 19, 1978.
36. J. Richard Crout, *The Nature of Regulatory Choices,* Center for the Study of Drug Development, University of Rochester Medical Center, Rochester, New York, January 1978, p. 10.

8

The Public Response:
The Need for
Greater Understanding

Beneficium invito non datur.
(A benefit cannot be bestowed on an un-
willing person.)
Old Latin maxim

AS shown in the preceding two chapters, business and government have key and obvious roles in dealing with the problems
that arise from the vast amount of government intervention in
the private economy. But the fundamental pressures for the expansion of government have come from other areas, from a wide
assortment of interest groups and academic sources augmented
by the nation's rich variety of communications media. In this
chapter, attention will be focused on the latter institutions, which
in their totality often serve as a proxy for the public interest.

THE VARIOUS INTEREST GROUPS

Until the middle of the twentieth century, most of the interest
groups that were involved in advocating changes in business-
government relations were what could be called producer groups.
The public debates were dominated by business firms, trade associations, labor unions, and farmer organizations, all concerned

with some aspect of economic activity. In contrast, a newer type of interest group has tended to be the most prominent factor in public policy discussions in more recent years. The newer interest groups have concerns that are essentially social, and for that reason they are usually oblivious to the economic impacts of their proposals. They range from ecological associations to civil rights organizations to consumer groups. Many of them, especially in the legal area, have appropriated the very term "public interest group," and as a consequence their views tend to be reported as representative of the views of the citizenry as a whole.

Their claim to represent the public is not based on their knowledge of what the public wants or their accountability to the public. Instead, they implicitly assume that they know what is best for the consumer. Examples of the gap between the desires of the public and the actions of the self-styled public interest groups are numerous. Although most polls of the American consumer show that the majority prefer information about potential product hazards rather than bans, the activist consumer groups—ignoring the old maxim quoted at the head of this chapter—continue to urge the outright prohibition of products that they contend are "unsafe."

In addition, although 61 percent of consumer activists were reported to favor more government regulation of business, according to pollster Louis Harris and Associates, only 30 percent of the public share that view. A large majority of the public, 57 percent, either advocate less regulation or are content with the status quo.[1] Surely, these groups do represent the views of some significant portion of American consumers. The point made here is that, although they have an important constituency, it is obvious that they represent only a portion of the public.

The gap between public desires and the proposals of public interest groups can be seen in the attempt by Ralph Nader and his associates in late 1977 to organize a consumer group (FANS, or Fight to Advance Our Nation's Sports) to represent the "sports-consuming public." That effort resulted mainly in a field day for newspaper columnists. According to FANS, sports fans have a right "to be informed about the operations" of teams, to "participate in the formation of rules," and to have their interests "represented in contract disputes between players and owners."

In his column on this newest consumer group, George F. Will stated, "FANS is like many other organizations that are concocted by 'consumerists' skillful at making work for themselves. It is the assertion, by a few persons who have appointed themselves to speak for many strangers, of concerns that few consumers share." Mr. Will also referred to "comic consumerism," such as FANS, as part of the spread of public interest lobbies that provide "political make-work."[2]

Mike Royko was even more blistering in his comments on FANS:

> Nader seems to be having weird thoughts about what society's real problems are. . . . Apparently, Nader doesn't understand what the average sports fan really wants. . . . Anybody who thinks that the issue is the quality of hot dogs is square enough to believe that all those fans are betting bubble gum cards.[3]

Those responses illustrate the fact that one of the necessary tasks in improving public policy is to get the self-styled, self-appointed public interest groups to undergo a fundamental metamorphosis and broaden their intellectual horizons. Just listen to the plaint of the Public Interest Economics Foundation (an activist consumer-oriented group comprised of economists). Lee Lane of the Foundation's staff shows how the change advocated here is sorely needed:

> One of the most difficult problems faced in public interest lobbying is how to communicate basic economic principles without antagonizing consumer and other public interest groups who may not have taken them into consideration in formulating their position.[4]

All in all, the public, the media, and government decision makers must realize that a limited viewpoint prevents the typical public interest group from effectively representing the totality of the public interest. One of the groups' powers is the myth of their powerfulness. One might turn an old phrase in this case and refer to the "power of arrogance."

Walter Brueggemann, academic dean at Eden Theological Seminary, has referred to "coercive consumerism." In that regard, the power of consumer groups should not be underestimated. On June 15, 1978, Consumers Union labeled a Chrysler Corporation product (the Dodge Omni and the similarly designed Plymouth Horizon) as "the most unfortunate car of the year." Sales of the cars dropped off soon after that single action, even though the authoritative *Motor Trend* magazine earlier had named those two cars jointly as "Car of the Year." Chrysler reported a 23 percent decline for the 10-day period from June 20 to June 30 compared to sales for the last ten days of the preceding month. Subsequently, the government's own National Highway Traffic Safety Administration, after exhaustive testing, gave the cars a clean bill of health and stated that the Consumers Union tests bore "no significant relationship to any real-world driving task or maneuver." [5] But the damage had been done.

At times, even the liberal academic constituency of the public interest groups tends to grow impatient with the groups' economic illiteracy. Professor David Vogel of the School of Business Administration of the University of California at Berkeley (who could not be categorized as conservative by any stretch of the imagination) cited the shortcomings evident in a recent book on the corporation by Ralph Nader and his associates:

> The idea that there might be trade-offs between various economic and social objectives appears utterly foreign to its authors. They are unwilling to establish priorities. Their credibility is dangerously weakened when they glibly assure us that through appropriate legal changes, the corporation can be made to give us everything we want: cheap and safe products, high domestic employment, reduced air and water pollution, and continuous technological innovation. This legal determinism is economically naive. . . . I wish he [Nader] would make it easier for those of us who share his goals to defend his analyses.[6]

Vogel's remark may remind us that it is a platitude to state that communication is a two-way street. But the self-styled public interest groups do tend to act as if communication were strictly a one-way affair. They expect business firms to listen carefully to and respond rapidly to their "demands," but they cavalierly dismiss the points made by any business official as mere self-serving apologetics. That double standard is more than unfair; it makes the achievement of good public policy difficult.

The issues at stake are far too central to the future of American society to be dealt with by humoring or placating the attackers of the U.S. business system or by waiting until the attackers lose interest and pick on some other target. The problem is not one for business alone. The business system—unintentionally and surely not by choice—constitutes the front line of defense for consumers, homeowners, motorists, investors, employees, and taxpayers. Each of those groups (as we have seen) can be adversely affected by government action against business that is advocated by "corporate activists," who view the business firm as an instrument for achieving their social objectives.

The fiction that business does not care about people because profit comes first should be exposed for the errant nonsense that it is. Business has all the incentives to take actions that result in improving human welfare. The reasons for doing so arise, of course, not out of benevolence but out of hard-nosed, practical, and effective economic incentives. More purchases by willing consumers do tend to generate more profits and greater accumulation of capital. In the case of the self-appointed social activists, the situation is just the reverse. The social activists do not care about, or at least do not understand, the ultimate consequences of their actions. Knowingly or not, they would use the accumulated wealth of our society as their intellectual plaything.

Those are harsh words. But it is clear that a little humility would go a long way in reducing the shrillness of many of the representatives of the so-called public interest groups. It is no simple task to identify *the* public interest in any specific issue of public policy. To any participant in government policy making it is apparent that good policy consists of properly balancing and reconciling a variety of worthy interests. That is far more difficult than merely choosing, in a simple-minded fashion, between "public" or "consumer" interests, which are presumably good and to be endorsed, and "special" or business interests, which are presumably evil and to be opposed.

To be sure, there is considerable variety among the various public interest groups. Some of the older consumer organizations and their publications are becoming aware of the adverse economic impacts of government intervention. For example, in the July 1978 issue, *Consumers' Research Magazine* reports that "Government regulations are raising the price of consumer products. There is a trend gaining in consumers' field of attention that involves evaluating cost vs. the benefits of so-called consumer legislation."

As stated in Chapter 1, the problem with the so-called public interest groups is not their venality but their belief that they alone represent *the* public interest. The confidence these groups have had in pursuing their numerous and sometimes far-reaching missions is not always warranted, especially when their activities— and their demands—are scrutinized in the context of the full effects of the government regulations which they so often instigate or endorse with tremendous zeal. To be sure, it is commonplace for members of various groups—including trade associations and labor unions—to identify their interests with the national interest. But unlike the public interest groups, the grandiose claims of those other organizations are usually dismissed as too obviously self-serving.

The shortcomings of these groups may not be so obvious, but they exist. For example, such groups are often tempted to try to protect people from themselves. A good example is the state laws requiring people riding motorcycles to wear helmets. When Colorado repealed the statute making helmets compulsory for motorcyclists, helmet use declined substantially and injuries and deaths rose dramatically. Between 1976 and 1977, the proportion of cycle accidents in that state involving severe head injuries rose 260 percent and the rate of deaths climbed 57 percent.[7]

Why did Colorado, and 21 other states, eliminate the compulsory helmet laws? Primarily because of the pressure from the cyclists themselves, who contended that such rules infringe their personal rights. So, should adults be permitted to take risks which may be lethal? Or should the government overrule their individual judgment? Such difficult philosophical questions may stimulate great cocktail party conversations. ("If society is going to protect individuals from their own folly, why limit the action to cyclists? Why not include tobacco smoking, heavy eating, excessive drinking, and so on?")

But such philosophical approaches ignore the wide range of intermediate positions in which more satisfying solutions may be found. Informed consumers, for example, may be less prone to take high risks than those who are not aware of the true nature of the hazard. Rather than choose between the alternatives of doing nothing and taking the route of compulsory safety, government might follow the intermediate position of making information on motorcycle hazards more readily available to cyclists. The choice of wearing a helmet or not would be made by the individual, but it might be a more informed choice than is now being made.

Moreover, public interest groups, as well as regulatory decision makers, tend to ignore the fact that many individuals voluntarily engage in hazardous activities which are not necessarily economic in nature. According to the American Industrial Health Council, the following are the risks associated with typical recreational pursuits. It is intriguing to note that many of the categories, which are basically unregulated, are on the average far more hazardous than many of the highly regulated activities in which people engage to earn a living.

Activity	Annual Projected Deaths Per 100,000 Participants
Motorcycle racing	180
Horse racing	130
Automobile racing	100
Rock climbing	100
Canoeing	40
Power boating	17

By way of comparison, the comparable figure for manufacturing industries is 8 deaths per 100,000 workers.[8]

It is not inevitable, of course, that public interest groups remain oblivious to the desires of consumers who want less rather than more government intervention in private matters. The public interest (PI) phenomenon took a new twist in the 1970s. The supporters of the private enterprise system, who for years have seen environmental activists and other PI groups inhibit or terminate business operations, have now turned the tables on those same groups by using comparable or identical legal methods. The numerous new groups, working in opposition to the "traditional" PI organizations, act as clearinghouses for research and litigation and attempt to bring a sense of balance to matters pertaining to that broad and elusive term, "the public interest."

The first of the "new breed" of public interest groups was the Pacific Legal Foundation, an independent law firm established in Sacramento in 1973. Its founders sought to counter the force of a small group of citizens who, ostensibly acting on behalf of the public at large, had delayed year after year the Trans-Alaska pipeline, offshore drilling for oil and gas, and other vitally needed energy resources on what the Foundation considered to be the most specious of environmental criteria. Similar groups subsequently have been set up in other regions of the country. The Southeastern Legal Foundation is based in Atlanta; the Mid-America Legal Foundation in Chicago; the Great Plains Legal Foundation in Kansas City; the Mid-Atlantic Legal Foundation in Philadelphia; the Mountain States Legal Foundation in Denver; the Northeastern Legal Foundation in Springfield, Massachusetts; and the Capital Legal Foundation in Washington, D.C.

The regional PI law centers have joined in or initiated a variety of lawsuits that challenge the legal actions taken by older PI groups. Increasingly, the newer law foundations have found that federal and state environmental laws and other regulations need not necessarily be the bane of business but can on occasion be used to the advantage of the private sector. The various causes in which the groups have taken part, often in *amicus curiae* (friend of the court) briefs, include the snail darter case previously discussed, use of West Coast ports for Alaskan oil, and OSHA's authority to conduct inspections of businesses without search warrants. The latter resulted in a Supreme Court decision requiring search warrants.[9]

The Pacific Legal Foundation filed suit requesting that the Environmental Protection Agency prepare an environmental impact statement prior to banning DDT. The Foundation charged that the risks involved in using the pesticide against the tussock moth were negligible compared to the damage done by the insect to timber (the moths destroy about 700 million board feet of wood each year). The case was settled when the EPA dropped its opposition and granted a DDT permit.[10]

The new breed of PI organizations is now also active in the health field. The American Council on Science and Health was set up in July 1978 to compete with Ralph Nader's Health Research Group and Center for Science in the Public Interest. According to Dr. Elizabeth Whelan, the founder of the new council, "What we object to is the current tendency to call 'cancer' at just the slightest evidence, and the eagerness of our government regulatory agencies to ban perfectly useful substances at the hint of hypothetical risk."

The rise of this new breed of public interest groups points, in short, to the numerous shortcomings of the older groups. In large measure, the rise was necessitated by the unwillingness of the self-appointed public interest organizations to take full account of the consequences of their actions, which was a result of their obliviousness to economic considerations. The advent of competition among public interest groups also was instigated by the overconfident belief of the older breed of public interest groups that they and they alone represented the public at large. People do not in all cases want to be protected from themselves; they usually want to make their own informed decisions. Nor do people always want to pay the hidden tax incurred by heavy governmental regulation of business. It is fairly clear, therefore, that the activists, now faced with a cogent and persuasive opposition, need to reassess their positions and their methods and the goals toward which they work—not merely for their own continued existence but, more importantly, for the interests of the public they wish to represent.

ACADEMIC RESEARCH

The need to improve understanding of the business-government interaction extends beyond the interest groups to the researchers in academia. There is, unfortunately, a parallel between generals fighting the last war and academic men and women researching issues of public policy: Many of them are behind the times. When business executives, labor union representatives, public interest groups, or government officials discuss government regulation of business, their key concerns relate to the newer cross-industry type of regulation typified by EPA, OSHA, EEOC, and CPSC. Yet academic research is still preoccupied with railroads, television, and airlines, which are the industries subject to the older, more traditional type of regulation.[11]

The point to be made here is not that the ICC, CAB, or FCC do not deserve professional attention. Instead, the point is that academic literature and teaching need to take fuller account of the expansion in scope and change in character of government regulation of business during the past decade. As we have seen, the expansion in regulation—whether measured by the size of regulatory budgets or by the numbers of rules—by and large is in the newer areas. The prevailing theories and models of regulation need to be reworked to take account of the revised institutional structure. Whether the railroads and their unions "capture" the Interstate Commerce Commission is a far more trivial concern than understanding the full range of impacts of environmental, safety, and employment regulation.

The traditional academic way of looking at government regulation is no longer appropriate. As pointed out in Chapter 7, the case is not so much that the standard theory of government regulation of business is obsolete; rather, it is that the theory is inappropriate for an increasing share of regulatory activity. The newer types of regulatory agencies do not conform to the standard theory, which, we may recall, was based on the industry type of regulatory commission such as the ICC. The key shortcoming of the new type of regulation is not that the regulated industries will "capture" the government agencies that regulate them; the main danger is that the proponents of the social regulations will be oblivious to the serious economic impacts of their demands. Although deregulation may often be the simple but effective solution to the problems of the older, industry-type regulation, the elimination of health, safety, and related regulation is neither warranted nor realistic. There is a great need for objective and analytical research focusing on ways to improve the effectiveness of the newer regulatory efforts and also reduce the many adverse side effects of regulation that we enumerated in earlier chapters.

Academic research could make an important contribution to the regulatory process by exploring the effective limits of regulation and identifying promising alternative methods of achieving public policy objectives. The administrative limits to regulation surely are a fit subject for future research. However, other and perhaps far more urgent limits arise from the adverse impact of the increasing government involvement in internal business decision making. That development can be termed a "second managerial revolution" because so many of the traditional prerogatives of corporate management are being taken over by an immense cadre of government planners, regulators, and inspectors.[12]

When in this regard we examine the sector of industry that already is most subject to government supervision—defense production—the results are disconcerting. It is precisely the companies, such as Lockheed, that are most heavily dependent on military contracts that report the largest cost overrun and the longest delays. Therefore, it is clear that the ultimate consequence of government assumption of basic entrepreneurial and managerial functions is surely a topic worthy of considerable attention and study. The undesirable characteristics of a "Lockheed economy" have not generally permeated civilian-oriented industries, but the experiences of that closely regulated and highly subsidized company surely provide some warning of what can happen nationwide.

Although we have focused on shortcomings and disagreements in academic thinking, it would be useful to remind the public of the wide agreement that exists among professional economists on many of the issues discussed in this book. In his presidential address to the American Economic Association, Walter Heller (an outstanding economist with impeccably liberal credentials) stated:

> Economists widely, in some cases almost uniformly, favor tougher antitrust policy, freer trade, deregulation of transportation, pollution taxes in place of most prohibitions. . . . They oppose fair trade laws, restrictive labor and management practices, distortive zoning laws and building codes, import quotas, ceilings on interest rates.[13]

Heller's view is indeed widely held among the academic economists. Professor James Tobin of Yale (another former president of the American Economic Association and also a well-known liberal) stated matter-of-factly in a recent book review, as if he were reporting a warm day in July: "Business and the consuming public are victims of excessive and mindless regulation." [14]

To show the extent of the agreement that now exists between supposedly "liberal" and supposedly "conservative" economists on the issue of government regulation, here are two statements (made in 1962) by Nobel laureate Milton Friedman, who is perhaps the dean of economic "conservatives":

> At any moment in time, by imposing uniform standards in housing, or nutrition, or clothing, government could undoubtedly improve the level of living of many individuals; by imposing uniform standards in schooling, road construction, or sanitation, central government could undoubtedly improve the level of performance in many local areas and perhaps even on the average of all communities. But in the process, government would replace progress by stagnation, it would substitute uniform mediocrity for the variety essential for that experimentation which can bring tomorrow's laggards above today's mean.

In short, Friedman contends that "what we urgently need, for both economic stability and growth, is a reduction of government intervention, not an increase." [15]

Finally, we should note the strong intellectual agreement on the fundamentals of the capitalistic system. The following statement by a thoughtful liberal economist, Robert Heilbroner, is one that most conservative economists would be pleased to endorse:

> Freedom in the sense that we use the word to describe our political, economic, and social liberties is a bourgeois idea, indissolubly linked to the celebration of the individual that underpins the culture of capitalism.[16]

It is one thing for academics to be in such widespread agreement on matters related to the fundamental nature of this nation's economic system. It is quite another thing, however, for the public to understand that the agreement exists. Bridging the gap between the two is a challenge to the media, and in good measure, so far, it is an unmet challenge.

THE NEGLECTED ROLE OF THE MEDIA

The author once attended a meeting of business executives addressed by the publisher of one of the nation's major newspapers. That publisher expressed her great concern about the economic illiteracy of the American public; she cited the large difference between what the average member of the public thinks corporate profits are (a rather large number) and what the profits actually are (a much lower number).[17] No one in the audience was so impolite as to ask the lady the obvious question, "Where did she think the public obtained such inaccurate information about American business?"

The answer is complex, of course; it involves the formal system of education, the various interest groups, and business firms themselves. But to a very large degree the question itself implicates the communications media—the newspapers, magazines, books, and radio and television stations, which provide Americans with the great bulk of their information and ideas on all sorts of matters, including issues of public policy.

Louis Banks, former managing editor of *Fortune* and now a teacher at MIT, described how, when he started teaching an advanced course for business executives, he first learned the depth of emotion felt by corporate executives about the media's coverage of business: "One of the reasons journalists don't know [about that depth of emotion] is that few businessmen . . . are brave enough to speak out openly for fear of retaliation." [18] In a comment on Banks's point, Kevin Phillips, a nationally syndicated columnist himself, compared some journalists to the members of the court of France's Louis XVI in the 1780s: "They don't care what's happening out in the provinces." [19]

On the other hand, here is what one writer who edited a national business weekly for several years and subsequently spent 17 years in public relations has to say on this matter:

> I don't understand *everything* media people do. Reporters and editors, like even corporate executives . . . sometimes have a bad day and do off-the-wall things. . . . Just as a small minority of business executives dispensed illegal or improper campaign contributions, so too there is a relatively small percentage of lazy or sleazy journalists. By far the greater number of journalists are reasonable people willing to listen to anyone they consider credible and whose opinions are supported by facts.[20]

All in all, there is great variation in media coverage of business and economic affairs. Some journalists have become veritable experts in reporting and analyzing current developments in those fields. Their work is properly relied upon as source information by scholars and government officials alike. Far more writers on business and related topics, however, lack a basic comprehension of the activities that they are reporting on. No sports desk would ever assign a reporter to cover a baseball game if he was unfamiliar with the rules of the game. But a comparable level of competence is not a general requirement for covering an annual meeting of a major corporation or for reporting on a critique of business by an important interest group. To worsen the situation, any criticism of the inaccurate coverage more often than not will provoke a diatribe on attempted interference with the freedom of the press.

It surely is not a question of accountability to business; it is a matter of responsibility to the public for fair and informed reporting on any major sector of the society. By no means is that a plea for business to use its advertising budget to influence the coverage that it receives by the media. To restate the obvious, that would be both morally reprehensible and counterproductive. Stanley Marcus, who headed the Neiman Marcus department stores for years, offers the following admonition: "A businessman can make no worse mistake than to try to use the muscle of his advertising dollar to try to influence the news." [21]

Frankly, it is disheartening to see the public fed, and coming to expect, a steady diet of biased reporting. Here is a minor but frequently encountered example: The staff of the SEC is drafting regulations that would require corporations to use a more uniform system of reporting compensation. How is that reported? As another increase in the reporting burden on business? Hardly. Here is the lead sentence in the article on the subject in the July 3, 1978, issue of *The Wall Street Journal:* "The Securities and Exchange Commission staff is preparing a further crackdown on the way publicly held companies report their executives' compensation." How can the typical reader avoid getting the impression that business is doing something so shady that it warrants a "crackdown" by government? *The Wall Street Journal* has a deserved reputation for the excellence of its reporting, and it is true that the patient reader of that article will get a fuller and more dispassionate report in the body of the article. But the reportorial approach is what is being criticized here.

Another example of that bias, also no doubt unintentional, occurred during the period of energy problems in 1974. When an oil company reported increased profits, it was front page news. When a company in another industry strongly affected by the energy situation (automobiles) revealed a decline in profits, the item appeared behind the sports section somewhere on the financial page. It is not surprising that many citizens began talking about business "rip-offs." That incident also shows a key shortcoming of most efforts to increase the economic understanding of reporters: the efforts tend to be aimed primarily or solely at business and financial writers. In newspapers and even more urgently in radio and television, it is the general news reporters who usually are least informed about business matters—and from whom the general public obtains most of its information and impressions about what is happening in and to American business.

The situation will not fundamentally improve until the average reporter stops thinking in simple-minded stereotypes, such as "Big business is a collection of fat cats trying to rip off the public" and "Public interest groups are the white knights who are protecting the public from that rip-off." The reporter should be equally suspicious of *all* advocates in the public policy arena. A contention does not become a fact just because it is uttered or written by a self-styled consumer advocate—or even by a college professor.

Moreover, reporters should have some understanding of the implications of their *own* actions. Kevin Phillips provides some interesting though controversial ideas in this regard:

> By promoting alienation with the present economic system, advocacy journalists are indirectly promoting growth of the state. In confirmation, all one has to do is think about the dissatisfactions and causes fanned by the media. . . . All have involved the creation of bureaucracy, of new layers of government, of new taxes.[22]

Surely the responsibility for communicating to the public a far better understanding of the business system and the impact on it by government falls on the shoulders of the journalism profession. It is not appropriate for business to play the "heavy" and to seek out reporters and try to convince them that they need to learn more about the business world. Business-sponsored courses in "economic journalism" may be a useful first response. But, realistically, the initiative must be reversed: the journalism profession should willingly see the need for broadening the intellectual horizons of its members and seize the initiative themselves. Journalists should be knocking on the doors of business, academia, and elsewhere in an attempt to gain that understanding of the vital part of the American society that is the business system.

When we read the growing body of literature on media coverage of business, it is apparent that one vital but neglected distinction must be made: the distinction between (1) business's complaints about adverse or critical news reporting and (2) the concern of business and indeed of the rest of society over inaccurate and misleading reporting. The gripes on the part of business executives about the excessive amount of criticism that they receive in newspapers, magazines, and on radio and television can be dismissed quickly. Marshall Loeb, senior editor of *Time,* reminds us that we are living in an era when all institutions are under fire—the church, government, the press, medicine. "Business," he notes, "is attacked more than many other institutions because it is highly visible." [23]

But it is the second concern, dealing with inaccuracy in the media, that deserves serious attention. According to the chief executive of one of the nation's largest companies, here is the response he got from a nationally syndicated columnist when he called some errors to the columnist's attention: "Sorry about the errors, but so what? You should not get upset when you're attacked." [24]

There is no excuse for uncorrected errors, and no segment of society, business or any other, should be expected to be at the receiving end of inaccurate reporting without responding. Criticism of our institutions, business included, is of course proper— and highly desirable. Giving the public inaccurate information is neither proper nor desirable. When a layman points that out, he should not in turn be lambasted by reporters for trying to interfere with the freedom of the press. Louis Banks describes this phenomenon as follows:

> Most of my friends who write, edit, publish, or broadcast the news work behind an invisible shield . . . of righteousness, defensiveness, and self-protection which blocks out germs of conflicting judgment or thoughtful criticism from other elements of our world.[25]

Lewis Young, editor-in-chief of *Business Week,* also has observed "a lack of understanding of how business works by newspaper reporters, since most have never worked in a business." [26] In the author's own experience with the media, the great majority of journalists are deeply concerned with accuracy of reporting and fairness in coverage (although they may not always achieve those objectives). As Katherine Graham, the publisher of the *Washington Post,* has pointed out, "The ordinary is not noteworthy. . . . The occasional business failure or the isolated crime makes headlines; there are no stories when products are delivered on time, when soup is safe, when candy bars don't shrink." [27]

But then again there is a fine line between vigorous coverage of important events and taking that "step beyond." The distinguished journalist and historian Theodore White, author of a series of books on recent presidential elections, noted the dilemma in fairly colorful language:

> You don't make your reputation as a reporter, and I did not make my reputation as a reporter, by praising anybody. You make your reputation as a reporter by gouging a chunk of raw and bleeding flesh from this system. . . . You gotta be able to prove you can snap your jaws for the kill. But maybe we've gone too far and maybe there should be someone to call us to account for this also. [28]

A business viewpoint similar to White's was expressed by Donald MacNaughton, at one time the chairman of the Prudential Life Insurance Company: "Sixty seconds on the evening news tonight is all that is required to ruin a reputation . . . or impair a company's profitability. The power of the press with today's methods of mass communication has become . . . the power to destroy." [29]

This is not a plea for any outsider to call the journalism profession to account, to use White's phrase; rather, it is a matter for self-restraint. Just as the adverse reaction to the slush fund scandals resulted in a *voluntary* improvement in the prevailing mores of the business system, so a similar realization is required by members of the journalism profession. Sensationalism and colorful but inaccurate phrases may help to get an article into a publication and into a more prominent location (laymen tend to ignore the keen competition that exists among reporters for a given newspaper or TV station). But such action should come to be considered beyond the bounds of good journalism. As Irving

Kristol has written, most journalists may not "give a damn" what the business community thinks of them, but they care very much about the kind of professional reputation they have among their peers.[30]

IMPROVING PUBLIC UNDERSTANDING

As pointed out at this chapter's start, the three major groups discussed here—the interest groups, the academic researchers, and the reporters in the media—often serve in their totality as a proxy for the public interest. That is, each of those private groups has sufficient power to influence the public policies which affect, in so many ways, the people of this nation.

If that is true—and it would appear to be—then the unifying theme that underlies the responses of each of the groups is the interesting and difficult notion of "representation" in the broadest sense of the word. Each of the groups has the power to influence what happens to citizens simply because each, to varying degrees, has acquired the power to stand in the citizens' place and to speak for the citizens. Each can "re-present," or "present again," *for* the people what each perceives to be the desires and opinions *of* the people. Such power is by no means negligible.

But given that line of reasoning, the implications for the roles of public interest activists, academicians, and reporters are profound. The implications involve, first of all, the perceptions of each group, that is, what each group perceives to be truly "public" opinions and desires. They also involve what each group perceives to be the function of government and the proper role of business. We may find those perceptions have a common ground when we consider them in light of the hard facts about the unintended and often adverse effects of government regulation.

Second, the implications of the groups' roles involve the critical concept of responsibility. Each group, since it possesses power, has the obligation to respond constructively to the issues in government policy which affect the lives of the people the group represents. Each of the groups, for that reason, must be willing to do a number of things: (1) improve its understanding of its own role in society, whether it is raising the public consciousness or doing research or reporting to the public, (2) be more self-critical and self-restrained, (3) analyze more carefully both the short-term and the long-term effects of what it does and of the government actions it proposes, and, last but not least, (4) comprehend that government intervention in private activities inevitably "regulates," in a far different sense, the life of the nation's citizens for good or for ill.

A basic improvement in public policy toward the American business system is not a matter that can be handled by government and business alone. In our society, it is a matter that must be dealt with by interest groups, academicians, members of the media, and others who have the power, the perceptivity, the willingness, and the responsibility to represent the public and promote the public's interests.

References

1. Humphrey Taylor, "The Performance of the Consumer Movement," *Electric Perspectives,* No. 1 (1976).
2. George F. Will, "Sports Consumers, Beware of FANS," *Washington Post,* October 2, 1977.
3. Mike Royko, "Sports Consumers Group: Idea Off Sides?" *St. Louis Post-Dispatch,* October 17, 1977.
4. "PIE Lobbying," *Public Interest Economics,* December 15, 1976.
5. "No Problem Found in Chrysler Omni/Horizon Handling," *U.S. Department of Transportation News,* July 7, 1978; Ernest Hosendolph, "U.S. Agency Defends Two Chrysler Cars," *The New York Times,* July 8, 1978.
6. David Vogel, "Under the Corporate Thumb," *Working Papers,* Summer 1977.
7. "Rise in Cycle Deaths Is Linked to Repeal of Helmet-Use Laws," *The Wall Street Journal,* June 30, 1978.
8. American Industrial Health Council, *AIHC Recommended Alternatives to OSHA's Generic Carcinogenic Proposal* (Scarsdale, N.Y.: 1978), pp. 27–28.
9. *Legal Activities Reporter* (Washington, D.C.: National Legal Center for the Public Interest, 1978), pp. i–vi.
10. G. Christian Hill, "Turning the Tables: Businesses Are Finding

Environmental Laws Can Be Useful to Them," *The Wall Street Journal*, June 9, 1978.

11. For an interesting foray into developing a broader model of regulation, see Barry R. Weingast, *A Positive Model of Public Policy Formation: The Case of Regulatory Agency Behavior*, Working Paper No. 25 (St. Louis: Washington University Center for the Study of American Business, 1978).

12. See Murray L. Weidenbaum, *Business, Government, and the Public* (Englewood Cliffs, N.J.: Prentice-Hall, 1977), pp. 285–287.

13. Walter W. Heller, "What's Right with Economics?" *American Economic Review*, March 1975.

14. James Tobin, "Treasurer's Report," *The New York Times Book Review*, June 11, 1978.

15. Milton Friedman, *Capitalism and Freedom* (Chicago: University of Chicago, 1962), pp. 4, 38.

16. Robert L. Heilbroner, "Capitalism, Socialism, and Democracy," *Commentary*, April 1978.

17. Katherine Graham, "Business and the Press," *University of Michigan Business Review*, January 1976.

18. Louis Banks, "Taking on the Hostile Media," *Harvard Business Review*, March–April 1978.

19. Kevin P. Phillips, "Why Many People Are Turning Against the Media," *Enterprise*, May 1978.

20. John L. Poluszek, *Will the Corporation Survive?* (Reston, Va.: Reston, 1977), pp. 224, 231.

21. Stanley Marcus, quoted in Louis Banks, "Memo to the Press: They Hate You Out There," *Atlantic*, April 1978.

22. Phillips, op. cit., p. 10.

23. Quoted in S. Prakash Sethi, "Business and the News Media," *California Management Review*, Spring 1977.

24. "Business and the Press," *Management Review*, July 1977.

25. Louis Banks, "Memo to the Press: They Hate You Out There," *Atlantic*, April 1978.

26. Sethi, op. cit., p. 54.

27. Graham, op. cit., p. 23.

28. Quoted in Poluszek, op. cit., p. 225.

29. Donald S. MacNaughton, "The Businessman Versus the Journalist," *The New York Times*, March 7, 1976.

30. Irving Kristol, *Two Cheers for Capitalism* (New York: Basic Books, 1978), p. 99.

9

The Future
of Business: Shock
or Stability?

There are no great solutions and as we
proceed we should do so cautiously . . .
but I do say we should proceed.
Roderick M. Hills
Former SEC Chairman

CLARENCE Walton, a distinguished student of business-government relations, concludes an essay on corporate ethics with the statement, " 'Life is not so simple' marks the beginning of ethical wisdom." [1] The admission that life is not so simple may also mark the beginning of wisdom in dealing with the development of public policy toward the business system. Leonard Silk, the economics columnist of *The New York Times,* writing in the same vein, reminds us that moral issues involve conflicts, not between "good" and "bad," but between "goods." [2] Perhaps that explains why an economist feels obliged to jump into the murky waters of public policy toward business—precisely because making such policy involves difficult choices among worthy alternatives.

The history of government intervention into private economic activity surely is replete with examples of regulations which were born of good intentions but which wound up being far more deadly than the disease they were supposed to cure. As we have seen in earlier chapters of this book, many government undertakings, such as those intended to improve the safety of products, may produce side effects that are far more worrisome such as lessened product variety, higher prices paid by the consumer, and on occasion newer and more dangerous product hazards. But as stated before, it is not a question of being for or against safer products or a healthier environment; neither, of course, is it a matter of being for or against inflation or unemployment. As in most matters in life, it is a question not of either-or but of more or less and how to choose among those "goods."

Both American business and the American public have been faced with more and more burdens imposed by government. The direct costs to business firms in complying with regulations certainly have been enormous, but by and large they get passed on to the consumer in the form of higher prices (which is no little cost, as we have seen). But the indirect costs that result when companies have to change their basic ways of operating—to survive in the ever-larger regulatory network—are of much greater long-term significance; those costs are bound to grow, at least on the basis of current government policy. Finally, the induced costs resulting from government regulation—reductions of industry's pace of innovation, of its ability to grow and provide jobs for an expanding population, and of its basic capacity to produce goods and services for the public—far exceed any monetary quantity when they are compared with their effect on our overall *quality* of life. And literally to add insult to injury, those regulatory efforts—as we have seen—far too frequently just do not work. It is hardly a question of placing a dollar value on human life when the dollars spent for regulation often fail to attain the stated objective of saving lives or helping people.

Within the business system itself, government at all levels has had pervasive impacts on every type of private enterprise from the largest to the smallest. We might say that in the past decade exotic colors have been added to what was already a bizarre rainbow of government interventions in the private sector. American business faces a future that could be pessimistic if the growth of government power over business continues at the current rate. But it is surely within our means to opt for a bright future, one characterized by restraint in the use of government regulation.

The optimistic scenario is possible if at least three key tasks are performed. First of all, American business will have to take a number of important but difficult steps in improving its day-to-day relations with the public sector. That includes dismantling what we have referred to as the imperial presidency in the private sector. Second, government will have to exercise more self-restraint in, and more self-criticism of, its multitude of regulatory actions. Government officials will have to adopt more sympathetic views of their public responsibilities in their relations with business. Finally, public interest groups, academic researchers, and the media will have to work in their powerful ways to improve public understanding of the many implications of government policies toward the private sector of the economy.

The one-dimensional perspective on complex matters, which often describes the outlook of the so-called public interest organizations, is a failing that needs to be fully recognized and, hopefully, remedied. For example, those groups quite properly berate business and other traditional institutions for their preoccupation with economic goals to the exclusion of such other important needs of society as a healthy environment. But they themselves exhibit a similar, if not greater, preoccupation with a single social need, such as pure air or water, and forsake all other considerations. Interestingly enough, the public at large is surprisingly well aware of the complexity of reality and of the need for balance among important and competing objectives.

Evidence for that awareness is not hard to find. In-depth polling of the American public by the Gallup organization and Potomac Associates provides interesting signals to all those who would attempt to influence and alter public policy. The polls show that the American people have the greatest "sense of progress" in overcoming some of the social problems (notably

environmental pollution and discrimination) which have motivated much of the recent wave of governmental regulation. But
in striking contrast, the public signals far less of a sense of progress in the economic problem areas (inflation and unemployment) which are exacerbated by the activities of the new regulatory agencies.

In 1976, for example, 68 percent of the public polled reported
a sense of progress in handling the problems of black Americans
and 63 percent in reducing water pollution. However, only 35
percent reported a sense of progress in controlling rising prices
and only 44 percent in dealing with the problem of unemployment.[3]

William Watts and Lloyd Free of Potomac Associates, the two
researchers who analyzed the Gallup data, point out two "unfortunate effects" that flow from the belief that 100 percent perfec-
tion in the environmental field should be sought in "an otherwise
imperfect world." The first is that the "superenvironmentalists"
(Watts's and Free's term) condemn themselves to frustration and
bitterness. The second adverse effect is that they turn on those
who recognize the need to strike the best possible compromise
between competing political, social, and economic demands and
then "vilify them as traitors to the cause." [4]

Surely a case can be made for some moderate shift of government attention from social to economic concerns. Here too the
public at large shows far more depth of understanding than the
often-shrill public figures who claim to represent it. The contrast
is evident in the resounding conclusion offered by Watts and
Free on the basis of their detailed analysis of American public
opinion: "The insistent call from Americans is to make the system
work more effectively, and to strengthen the bonds between the
leadership in our major institutions and the populace at large."
That is precisely the position advocated in Chapter 8. It is naive
to assume that the public interest groups—as well as business
and government—will voluntarily make changes of the kind out-
lined in the preceding chapters. Only a fundamental shift in
public opinion and an aroused citizenry will force them to do so.

THE FUTURE OF THE AMERICAN CORPORATION

In Chapter 1 we referred to the growing concern over whether the modern corporation will survive in the United States.[5] In a sense, two different answers can be provided to that question, one negative and one positive. From the negative aspect, the corporation as we know it today may not be the dominant private institution in the twenty-first century. But from the positive aspect, we might state with equal confidence that the corporation, with some substantial modifications, indeed is likely to continue to be the dominant institution in the private economy of the United States for another century.

Such optimism is not without firm foundation, for the modern corporation never has been a static or inflexible entity, and there is no reason to expect that it will become one. The typical American corporation is becoming more responsive to the needs of the society of which it is a part. For example, voluntary programs to bring minority groups into the mainstream of corporate life are both substantial and commonplace. Most business enterprises, however, are making sensible modifications intended to slough off the excesses that were often adopted during the late 1960s and early 1970s, when social responsibility became the "in thing." The current response is not due to any charitable impulse; it arises from a more sensible and durable motive: the instinct to survive and prosper by meeting more completely the needs and desires of the society of which business is a part.

Neil Jacoby of UCLA, a keen observer of the American corporation, has provided some useful conceptualization of the shift toward greater responsiveness. He sees the modern American corporation as adopting a "social environment" model in which the enterprise reacts to the total social environment and not merely to markets.[6] Quite clearly, both market and nonmarket forces can affect a firm's costs, sales, profits, and assets. Corporate behavior increasingly responds to political forces, public opinion, and government pressures, regardless of whether those factors are welcomed or helpful. No company can afford to ignore public attitudes and expectations—simply because to do so would result directly in loss of sales and customer goodwill or indirectly in increased costs to the extent that those pressures lead to further government intervention in business. The knowledge of that voluntary business response, firmly motivated by enlightened self-interest, should be a factor that interest groups and government decision makers increasingly take into account before proposing or implementing additional government involvement in the activities of the private sector of the economy.

Indeed, many companies have been instituting formal feedback processes designed to both inform management of changes in the external environment and encourage necessary changes in company policies and practices. Most firms have also embarked on the useful course of improving their channels of communication with employees, consumers, shareholders, students, religious and educational institutions, and other groups, many of which were considered in earlier times to be beyond the scope of business concern.

In viewing both recent and prospective developments in business-government relations, SEC Chairman Harold Williams has urged that the current emphasis in public policy should be on fostering private accountability, the process by which corporate managers are held responsible for the results of their stewardship. He sees that procedure as a preferred alternative to intervening directly in corporate governance to legislate a sort of federal "corporate morality." According to Williams, if corporations are to preserve the power to control their own destiny, they must be able to assure the public that they are capable of self-discipline.[7]

As we have seen in a variety of ways, those direct forms of government intervention in business decision making can often be self-defeating. Although business executives retain their nominal responsibility for "minding the store," their ability to actually do so is undermined by a host of government inspectors, regulators, and planners who increasingly are assuming aspects of traditional business responsibilities. In any event, the direct involvements by government in business usually have cumulative and serious adverse effects which were not intended by the proponents of the government action. Although Jeane Jordan Kirkpatrick (a political scientist at the American Enterprise Institute) was criticizing proposals to reform political party government, her views are strikingly relevant to the issues that we are dealing with here. She remarked: "It is a basic article of faith in the American creed that for every ill there is a remedy; by now experience . . . should have taught that, at least where political institutions are concerned, for every remedy there is probably an ill." [8] By exercising more self-restraint over the natural desire to improve private performance, government decision makers should give business a greater opportunity to do a better job of "minding the store."

If anything is clear from the analysis in this book of the growing government control of business decision making, it is the weakness—not the often-heralded strength—of business in the political process. After all, business generally has not urged the institution or the expansion of the new wave of regulatory agencies or programs. EPA, EEOC, ERISA, Tosca, CPSC, OSHA, and the rest of the regulatory "alphabet soup" generally were voted by Congress *despite* the strong opposition of the corporate community. That is not to say that business has no influence in the public arena; it is usually far more effective when it focuses its efforts on the specific programs that are advocated to benefit an individual industry (such as maritime subsidies and steel import quotas). But business is much less successful when it attempts to do battle on the broader issues which have led to the new wave of government intervention.

After reviewing business efforts on public policy issues, Neil Jacoby concluded in a 1977 study that business fought a defensive action against other interest groups, and that it usually failed. He adds, "There is also abundant evidence that, during the 1960s and early 1970s, corporate businesses were generally unable to bend federal administrative agencies to their will—contrary to the popular notion that they have 'captured' those agencies." Jacoby also contends that corporate political power reached its zenith during the nineteenth century and has ebbed gradually over the years—a contention which gives the lie to the assertions of public interest activists. "Today," Jacoby says, "it [business] is relatively less influential than ever. Far from being excessive, it may be too weak to maintain a vibrant market economy over the long run." [9]

GOVERNMENT AUTHORITY AND PRIVATE POWER

In the broad sweep of American history, the transcendent debate on ideology has been between the Jeffersonian and Hamiltonian approaches to democracy, which in effect relate to centralizing or decentralizing the power of government in society. To update that debate, the pertinent question now is how to allocate power between the individuals and voluntary institutions in the private sector on the one hand and the sovereign authority of government at all levels in the public sector on the other. In that regard, the author remains a patient optimist, believing that the now excessive power of the state will diminish as the balance of power shifts back gradually from the public sector to the private sphere. Perhaps the situation will worsen for a bit longer, however, before the public—thoroughly disenchanted with high taxes and big government—forces an improvement.

Because so many of the government actions affect business and thus are hidden from public view, we tend to forget how quickly and how far down the path of government control we have gone. In January 1965, Adolf Berle (co-author of the seminal work *The Modern Corporation and Private Property*) described the extent to which government had at that time limited the ability of business to use its "productive property." But, he added, "the state has not attempted (aside from police limitations) to tell a man what or how he should consume—that would constitute an intolerable invasion of his private life." [10] Obviously, however, Berle wrote prior to the compulsory installation of seat belts in the private automobile and before FTC proclamations on how much sugar we should have in our diet.

We are beginning to see the disenchantment with big government take the practical form of limits on state spending and taxing voted by aroused taxpayers. During the coming decade, it may also become increasingly apparent to the public that the aggregate effect of government regulatory actions is not the improvement of corporate performance. Instead, the result more often than not is, as we have seen, a marked reduction in the ability of the economic system to carry on its basic function: providing goods and services to the consumer.

What is likely to follow from that realization is not a dramatic series of moves to dismantle the bureaucratic apparatus which has been expanding so rapidly during the past two decades at all levels of government. There will not, in short, be a return to a simple status quo ante, since public concern with environmental quality, safety, equity, and similar social objectives will certainly remain. However, the *means* used to achieve the objectives may be changing drastically.

Many of the older regulatory programs, such as the ICC and their state counterparts, may be dismantled or at least cut back sharply in favor of reliance on competitive market forces. The focus of some of the newer regulatory agencies may be shifted from the promulgation of detailed standards to the use of incentives for private action, such as pollution taxes and a greater reliance on information provided to the consumer. The nearly universal adoption of and adherence to voluntary codes of business ethics should obviate the need for much of the compulsory controls over corporate governance that currently are being advocated with increasing vehemence.

Surely the state has not begun to wither away. That much is exceedingly clear. Nevertheless, the portion of the nation's resources being preempted by government, which has been rising in recent years, may begin to decline. That will permit a larger flow of private saving to corporate investment, thus obviating the need for many of the historic tax, expenditure, and credit subsidies to specific industries and geographical regions. Federal, state, and local governments may wind up doing less *to* and *for* business than is now the standard experience.

In the process, the various public interest groups will have to undergo an important metamorphosis. In turn, the public, the media, and government decision makers will have to realize that limited viewpoints prevent those public interest groups from effectively representing the overall public interest. A useful feedback may thus occur, with those groups acquiring a greater economic understanding. The change subsequently will generate an important force in gaining widespread acceptance of more positive departures in business-government relations.

In part, the more positive approach to public policy toward American business may be encouraged by a growing understanding of the international dimensions of business. American companies compete with increasingly powerful foreign enterprises in both domestic and foreign markets. Many of those foreign enterprises, rather than being restricted by their governments, are often subsidized by, if not actually a part of, the government apparatus. Not too surprisingly, U.S. shares of world trade have been declining steadily in recent years. The reasons are numerous, of course; they range from trade barriers overseas to higher costs of production at home. But employment and income in the United States surely suffer when the role of American business firms in the markets of the world is weakened, and public realization of the consequences should motivate positive responses in public policy.

To adopt that sanguine viewpoint at a time when the encroachment of government on business prerogatives is escalating may be reminiscent of Pollyanna's optimism or of Voltaire's Dr. Pangloss, who perennially saw his current environment as "the best of all possible worlds." That passive attitude surely is not the one advocated here. It will take a great deal of positive action, as well as difficult self-restraint, on the part of the many public and private groups and individuals involved to achieve the basic improvement in public policy envisioned here. Indeed, much of this book has been devoted to outlining those responsibilities for business, government, consumer and other interest groups, academic researchers, and those vital middlemen and women—the professionals in the communications media.

For those who despair of the likelihood of achieving such improvement, it may be fitting to end with a point made by William Carey, executive director of the American Association for the

Advancement of Science and one of the most incisive minds in the nation's capital. Carey draws a parallel between today's prophets of gloom and the *Nuremberg Chronicle* of July 14, 1493. That forecast of the imminent end of the world was made just when Columbus was approaching Lisbon with news of the discovery of the New World. As Carey puts it, "The heirs of the Nuremberg Chroniclers are still scribbling, still predicting the Seventh and last age of man, still discounting the possibilities of thought, discovery, and enterprise for giving tired and troubled institutions another chance." [11]

The American business firm, besieged by government regulators and private pressure groups, may indeed be tired and troubled. But when its contributions to material welfare and personal freedom are fully assessed, it surely deserves—and is likely to obtain—another chance from critics and supporters alike. The overriding theme of this book is that a reversal of the current trend of ever-increasing government intervention in business is essential not so much from the viewpoint of business, but primarily from the viewpoint of enhancing the welfare of the individual citizen.

References

1. Clarence Walton, ed., *The Ethics of Corporate Conduct* (Englewood Cliffs, N.J.: Prentice-Hall, 1977), p. 211.
2. Leonard Silk, "Moral Issues of Today's Economics," in *The Business System: A Bicentennial View* (Hanover, N.H.: Amos Tuck School of Business Administration, 1977), p. 23.
3. William Watts and Lloyd A. Free, *State of the Nation III* (Lexington, Mass.: Heath, 1978), p. 15.
4. Ibid., p. 103.
5. See Michael C. Jensen and William H. Meckling, "Can The Corporation Be Saved?" *MBA*, March 1977.
6. Neil H. Jacoby, *Corporate Power and Social Responsibility* (New York: Macmillan, 1973), pp. 192–195. See also George A. Steiner, *Business and Society* (New York: Random House, 1975).
7. Harold M. Williams, *Corporate Accountability*, an address to the

Fifth Annual Securities Regulation Institute (San Diego, Calif.: January 18, 1978), pp. 2, 14.

8. Jeane Jordan Kirkpatrick, *Dismantling the Parties* (Washington, D.C.: American Enterprise Institute, 1978), p. 31.

9. Neil H. Jacoby, "The Corporate State: Pure Myth," *Wharton Magazine*, Summer 1977.

10. Adolf A. Berle, "Property, Production and Revolution," *Columbia Law Review*, January 1965.

11. William D. Carey, "Technology and the Quality of Life," in *The Business System: A Bicentennial View* (Hanover, N.H.: Amos Tuck School of Business Administration, 1977), p. 70.

Index